Doing Business in Vietnam

Dr. Matthias Dühn

Doing Business in Vietnam

Vietnam Business Law for Foreign Investors and Entrepreneurs

Dr. Matthias Dühn, LLM (Georgetown)
Foreign Registered Lawyer, Vietnam

30A/32 To Ngoc Van Str., Tay Ho, Hanoi/Vietnam

ISBN: 978-3-910799-03-5
Publisher:

Design
The design of this paperback edition is based on the format template "Mindset" by Dominik Braun.

Consulting
„Mr. Bestseller“ Hartmut Paschke, www.hartmutpaschke.com

Dr. Matthias Dühn

Endorsement

Dear Investors and Entrepreneurs,

Vietnam has experienced a remarkable rise after its economic opening under the Doi Moi reforms (1986) and has developed from one of the poorest countries in the world into a dynamic powerhouse in the booming Asia-Pacific region. This is due to its integration into the global value chain, a clear commitment to free trade and investment protection and a largely market-based economy. Located in the centre of ASEAN and close to China, Vietnam is both an attractive trading partner and a prime location for foreign direct investment.

Nevertheless, there are challenges when entering the market. One or the other investment has usually run into rough waters due to a lack of detailed market research and due diligence. Expert legal advice is highly recommended for all business activities in Vietnam. I have known the author, Dr Matthias Dühn, since 2009, when I was a member of the Executive Board of Deutsche Bank Vietnam and he was Executive Director at the European Chamber of Commerce in Vietnam (EuroCham).

Since 2014, he and his Vietnamese partner have been successfully running Viet Diligence Legal, a lawfirm licenced in Vietnam. Matthias is qualified as a foreign registered lawyer with the Ministry of Justice in Hanoi and since then has acquired broad legal and business experience. In addition, he and his team of Vietnamese lawyers have developed over the years an incomparably broad network in Vietnam both in the public and the private sector.

Matthias has recorded in this guidebook his numerous practical experiences and challenges when dealing with legal issues in Vietnam. This practical guidebook is therefore highly recommended to all who are already doing business in Vietnam or are thinking of participating in Vietnam's future economic rise.

Prof. Dr. Andreas Stoffers

Country Director

Friedrich Naumann Foundation

Hanoi / Vietnam

Contents

Preface

Vietnam's real GDP grew by 8.0% in 2022, as the economy rebounded strongly from the economic disruption caused by the COVID-19 pandemic during second half of 2021. While economic growth has moderated in 2023, Vietnam remains an attractive destination for foreign investment, trade and doing business. Advantages of Vietnam include a stable economic and political environment, a skilled and comparatively low-cost workforce and an attractive domestic market which will cross the threshold of 100 million people by the end of 2023.

Since Vietnam's accession to the World Trade Organisation (WTO) in 2007, it has concluded 15 Free Trade Agreements (FTAs) with numerous countries, either individually or as a member of the Association of Southeast Asian Nations (ASEAN) and thereby further integrated into the world economy. In addition, Vietnam has completed FTA negotiations with Israel and is currently negotiating FTAs with Canada, the United Arab Emirates and EFTA (Switzerland, Norway, Iceland, Liechtenstein). A detailed list is available at: https://wtocenter.vn/thong-ke/13814-vietnams-ftas-summary-as-of-april-2019

The goal of this guidebook is to provide foreign investors and entrepreneurs with an overview of the legal framework for doing business in Vietnam. Even though Vietnamese laws have continued to improve over the years, investors and businesses, especially small- and medium sized enterprises, are still struggling with unnecessary bureaucracy and overly formalistic licensing and procedural requirements which are often caused by widespread corruption, particularly on the lower levels. In addition, while the quality of Vietnamese laws has improved over the years, government officials and agencies are often not sufficiently trained to correctly apply and interpret the laws in practice.

While this guidebook focuses on foreign direct investment and company formations, it also covers related legal matters such as taxation, HR and employment matters, IPR- and the newly emerging field of protection of personal data. While such a broad range of topics cannot be comprehensive or go into every conceivable detail, the guidebook wants to raise at least raise awareness that some matters could be problematic in practice and therefore need your attention. As there remains a pronounced difference between the "law in books" and the "law in action", I have included many examples and practical tips on how to practically deal with selected legal problems.

***

Disclaimer:

The information contained in this guidebook neither constitutes nor substitutes individual legal advice, because a short guidebook cannot analyze and consider the details of each potential case. In addition, laws and regulations in Vietnam are subject to frequent change. To improve future editions, we also welcome your feedback on structure, content and examples contained in this guidebook..

1. Introduction

1.1 Vietnam's Legal System

1.1.1 Hierarchy of Vietnamese laws

Since Vietnam's accession to the WTO in 2007, Vietnam has developed a modern legal system, with many laws having been introduced, modernized and sometimes completely renewed. However, as a side effect of Vietnam's rapid modernization of its legal framework, many conflicting and overlapping laws exist. This is aggravated by so-called "implementing regulations" such as Decrees, Circulars or Decisions, which in practice carry a much greater weight than the hierarchically superior laws passed by the National Assembly. Simplified, this hierarchy is as follows:

Legal Document	Issuing Institution
The Constitution	National Assembly
National Laws	National Assembly
Ordinances Resolutions	Standing Committee of the National Assembly Supreme People's Court
Decrees	Government
Decisions	Prime Minister
(Joint) Circulars	Ministries

Moreover, as Vietnamese legal education remains formalistic and administrative in nature, Vietnamese lawyers and legal practitioners are still struggling with legal methodology, specifically the interpretation of laws (legal methodology). Accordingly, Vietnamese courts and agencies will in practice mostly focus on the broad literal meaning of a legal term without taking into account its systematic order, its purpose and its historical context (thereby potentially interpreting it more narrowly than the literal meaning allows).

The Vietnamese legal system is largely based on statutory law (codified laws and regulations), while case law (precedent) is not binding legal authority. However, since the Supreme People's Court Resolution No. 03/2017/NQ-HDTP, Vietnam has been building a database of legal precedent, which will play an increasingly larger practical role in the future. According to Resolution No. 03 since 1st July 2017 certain judgments and decisions must be publicised within 30 days. These include - amongst others - first-instance judgments which have not been appealed or protested; appellate judgments; decisions on cassation and reopening in criminal, administrative, civil, marriage and family, business, trade and labour cases; decisions on settlement of civil matters.

Publication of above judgements happens on the "Electronic Judgments Portal" (https://congbobanan.toaan.gov.vn/otaticvn/ban-an-quyet-dinh). However, there are many types of decisions and judgments which are not permitted to be published.

1.1.2 Vietnamese Court System

The Vietnamese court system is four-tiered:

- The highest court is the Supreme People's Court.
- Three Superior People's Courts in Hanoi, Danang, and Ho Chi Minh City serve as appellate courts for specific case groups.

- 63 provincial-level People's Courts (both trial and appellate courts).
- District-level People's Courts are first-instance trial courts only.

In addition, military tribunals exist at various levels in the Vietnam People's Army, the highest being the Central Military Tribunal, which is subordinate only to the Supreme People's Court. The People's Procuracies - amongst other tasks - supervise and inspect compliance by courts and judges. For example, motions to replace judges can be filed here. For every People's Court, there is a People's Procuracy. The military has its own military procuracies, the highest being the Supreme People's Procuracy.

1.2 Judicial Enforcement

Vietnamese and recognized foreign judgment or arbitration awards are enforced in accordance with the Law on Enforcement of Civil Judgement, which lays out procedure, rights and limitations of the Vietnamese enforcement agency. Enforcement mechanisms in Vietnam are not yet comparable to western standards, although progress has been made in recent years. In addition, foreign parties face many obstacles specifically with regards to the enforcement of foreign judgments or arbitral awards.

Enforcement of foreign judgments: The enforcement of foreign judgments in Vietnam is practically difficult, because in principle, the recognition of foreign judgments in Vietnam is only possible if the foreign state has concluded an enforcement treaty or accord with Vietnam or reciprocity of enforcement is otherwise legally warranted, i.e., the foreign state acknowledges the corresponding Vietnamese judgments. Accordingly, foreign judgments are rarely enforced in Vietnam, except for those based on treaties. However, such treaties only exist between Vietnam and Algeria, Belarus, Bulgaria, Cuba, France, Hungary, Kazakhstan, Laos, North Korea, Poland, Russia, Ukraine, Cambodia, China, the Czech Republic, Slovakia, Mongolia and Taiwan.

Enforcement of foreign arbitral awards: Foreign arbitral awards, unlike VIAC arbitral awards, are also not automatically recognized by Vietnamese courts and enforcement agencies: Although Vietnam has been a member of the New York Convention on the Recognition and Enforcement of Foreign Arbitral Awards since 1995, Vietnamese courts and enforcement agencies often refuse immediate, automatic enforcement of foreign arbitral awards because of their potential violation of "*basic principles of Vietnamese laws*". Therefore, foreign arbitral awards must first be "recognized" by a Vietnamese court before they can subsequently be enforced by the Vietnamese enforcement agencies. In practice, foreign investors and entrepreneurs are therefore forced to conduct two different, subsequent procedural steps:

- First, the foreign arbitral award must be recognized by the competent court in Vietnam. Specifically, the court will double-check whether the award and its contents are "contrary to basic principles of Vietnamese laws". Also, the court will double-check whether all formalities have been adhered to in the original arbitration proceedings abroad. Although Vietnamese courts are becoming increasingly more favourable to the recognition and enforcement of foreign arbitral awards, the refusal rate for foreign award recognition is still quite high at 30-35%.

- Second, and only once the Vietnamese court has recognized the foreign arbitral award, procedures with regards to enforcing the (now recognized) award may be initiated.

Note: *Even where enforceability exists in principle, or where foreign judgments or awards are being recognized, Vietnamese contract partners often succeed in avoiding the foreign party's access to their company assets by moving or hiding assets to prevent proper enforcement, often assisted by enforcement agencies that are unduly influenced by those debtors.*

Foreign investors are therefore advised to settle disputes primarily by arbitration at the Vietnam International Arbitration Centre ("VIAC") at the Vietnamese Chamber of Commerce and Industry (VCCI). Agreeing with your Vietnamese business partner to arbitration at the VIAC has the advantage that that the VIAC's arbitral awards are not subject to the above recognition procedure and are thus directly enforceable in Vietnam. In addition, English can be agreed as the language to be used in arbitration proceedings at the VIAC, the parties can choose their arbitrators freely at the VIAC and the cost of VIAC proceedings are significantly lower than at the SIAC or other foreign arbitration centres. Accordingly, agreeing with your Vietnamese business on arbitration abroad is generally recommended only in exceptional and complex cases such as for example in multinational and/ or multijurisdictional disputes.

1.3 Selection of Business Partners

In Vietnam, the likelihood of encountering an untrustworthy contract partner is generally higher than in western countries. Therefore, foreign investors should thoroughly screen their potential business-, contract and joint venture (JV) partners in advance. This is particularly true for potential JV partners, because financially sound, commercially experienced and legally compliant Vietnamese JV partners are very hard to find. One reason for this is that most of the better potential JV partners have often found their foreign business partners already and are thus no longer actively looking for other or additional foreign JV partners. In addition, only a few potential JV partners have certain mandatory qualifications (specifically in terms of know-how, licenses and capital). This is particularly true where foreign investors are seeking for exclusive rather than non-exclusive JV or business partners. It is noteworthy that viable Vietnamese JV and business partners will expect the foreign investors' support in terms of training, marketing and distribution (including financial assistance). Therefore, JV and distribution contracts should address these matters carefully and detailed.

Once one or more potential JV partners are identified, the recommended background screening should identify amongst others the company's shareholders and management, use company-, audit- and external credit rating reports (where available), research information on the company's reputation and violations of the law in the past, and/or information about personal relationships to government officials. If the prospective JV partner poses a high risk, one should approach the potential JV partner to explain the due diligence findings.

1.4 Use of Intermediaries

Caution is required when including agents and or other intermediaries (e.g., brokers, dealers, customs agents or other "service providers") when doing business in Vietnam. As these intermediaries are formally and legally independent of the companies they advise, some foreign entrepreneurs and investors believe that their hiring is a smart way of avoiding certain doubtful or illegal business practices, particularly if these agents and intermediaries are used by business-, contract- or JV partners to facilitate the success of their investment project and/or to secure lucrative contracts.

Common cases include using agents and intermediaries as "deal brokers", "sales agents", "distributors" and "suppliers". In this context, payments will be made to an agent or broker to secure a lucrative contract or the opportunity to conclude a contract or enter a business relationship with a third party. The agent or broker, in turn, uses part of the fees paid to bribe these potential customers and/or business partners. Such payments are then often referred to as "special charges", "consulting fees" or "sales commission expenses" and recorded in the books of the company accordingly.

However, corruption cannot be outsourced and "accounting tricks" will often not remain undetected by the financial and tax authorities, which then poses a large legal risk to the foreign investor and his investment project in Vietnam. Therefore, while the use of agents and other intermediaries, as well as the payment of commissions, is not prohibited per se, they must be selected with the highest care and continuous supervision and monitoring.

If an intermediary is engaged, it should contractually commit to "act in full compliance with the applicable anti-corruption laws". The agreement with the intermediary should allow immediate contract termination if corruption occurs or seem likely. An audit right is useful in this context. To prevent corruption, activity reports should be mandatory, including specifically which activities the intermediary has performed at which cost. Fees for the intermediary's services must be at market rates, and any doubtful amounts should be carefully questioned.

1.5 Principles of Contract Law

1.5.1 Contents and Form Requirements

Art. 3 (2) of the Vietnamese Civil Code No. 91/2015/QH13, effective since 1st January 2017, explicitly recognizes the parties' rights to "*freely and voluntarily entering into commitments and/or agreements*" and therefore "*each commitment or agreement that does not violate regulations of law and is not contrary to social ethics shall be bound by the contracting parties and must be respected by other entities.*" For most civil matters, the referral to "social ethics" is practically not a problem, unless for example "sensitive" areas, such as trade in weapons, toxic waste, etc. are concerned. Overall, the contracting parties are therefore mostly free in their decision as to whether contracts should be concluded with whom and at what conditions.

In Vietnam, contracts can generally be concluded without adhering to specific form requirements, such as e.g. notarization. Exceptions exist for certain areas of the law, such as for example in family and real estate law, where official notarization is required for some contracts to be valid. For reasons of evidence and documentation, written form is strongly recommended even where no written form requirements exist. Such clause should specifically extend to amendmendts and changes to the contract. Furthermore, a written form clause is recommended in each contract in order to avoid objections of the other party that certain side agreements exist.

Although English is increasingly spreading in business transactions, Vietnamese remains the only official language both in legal documents and in Vietnamese courts. In practice, it is therefore advisable to always create bilingual versions of the relevant contracts and documentation. While it is in principle possible to have the English-language version prevail over the Vietnamese version, there are certain limitations if Vietnamese laws provide for the exclusive validity of the Vietnamese-language version (for example in certain family and real estate matters). If one contract party is a foreign party, and if both parties agree to arbitration at the Vietnamese International Arbitration Centre (VIAC), they may chose English-language proceedings at the VIAC.

The VIAC Model Arbitration Clause: *"The governing law of the contract is the substantive law of Vietnam. Any dispute arising out of or in relation with this contract shall be resolved by arbitration at the Vietnam International Arbitration Centre (VIAC) in accordance with its Rules of Arbitration. The place of arbitration shall be Hanoi, Vietnam. The language to be used in the arbitral proceedings shall be English. The award shall be binding on the parties."*

1.5.2 General Terms and Conditions

The use of "General Terms and Conditions" (GTCs) is becoming increasingly more widespread in Vietnam. There are no specific statutory regulations for GTCs, and therefore the admissibility of the use of GTCs results from above general contractual freedom of the parties. While certain limitations under consumer protection rules exist, these in most cases do not affect the use of GTCs if the other party agrees and/or is a commercial party. For reasons of evidence and to avoid disputes, it is recommended to include the GTCs in the form of an annex/appendix to the written individual contract (or order confirmation) with the Vietnamese contract partner, even though a simple link to the company's website (on which the GTCs are published) would be sufficient from a legal point of view.

For business transactions of a foreign-owned Vietnamese subsidiary with domestic Vietnamese customers the Vietnamese version of the GTCs will usually be binding, even though agreement on the English version is possible and potentially advantageous if arbitration at the VIAC is agreed on (see above). In practice, it is recommended to always make a bilingual English-Vietnamese version of the GTCs. While not mandatory, this can for example be useful if the FIE does not only have domestic but also cross-border transactions in the region. In that case, the GTCs can determine that the Vietnamese version prevails for domestic transactions while the English version governs cross-border transactions.

Important terms to include into GTCs are - amongst others - provisions on contract scope, payment terms including late payment or default, service/delivery terms such as time and place of performance, subsequent change of such service/delivery terms, consequences of partial and/or delayed performance, customer obligations, guarantees, liability for damages, indemnification, goods shipping and risk transfer, insurance requirements, contract termination, data protection, protection of intellectual property rights and dispute resolution. It is essential not to rely on templates but to seek individual advice for drafting the GTCs.

1.6 Common Drafting Mistakes

- ***Use of international (headquarters) contract templates:*** Headquarters of multinational companies often prefer to use their own contract templates for matters of internal (group) consistency in all jurisdictions they are active in. While this is understandable from a group point of view, at least local compliance with Vietnamese laws should be carefully checked. In addition, suitability of the template for the specific case should be reviewed, as no template can fully anticipate all details and specifics of the case at hand. An additional problem with international templates is that these are often very comprehensive and therefore too detailed for the Vietnamese side that generally works with simpler and shorter contract versions.
- ***Use of invalid contract templates:*** Sometimes, foreign investors use contract templates that are regarded as a circumvention of Vietnamese laws and are therefore invalid. This is for example true for so called "trustee" or "nominee" agreements with Vietnamese individuals if they intend to circumvent i) licensing requirements under the LOI or

ii) applicable maximum foreign ownership restrictions regarding shareholdings or holding of capital contributions in companies in specific business areas. In addition, for some areas of the law, certain Vietnamese templates exist. While not strictly legally binding, these should at least be considered both in form and content.

- ***Use of English contract versions only:*** If templates are used, they are often English-language only. While this is possible if dispute resolution at the VCCI is agreed, contracts in Vietnam should always be made in bilingual English-Vietnamese versions even where the English version could prevail and be basis for arbitration proceedings. If - however - no arbitration was agreed on and Vietnamese courts are therefore competent, the Vietnamese version will generally be prevailing.
- ***Carefully check the Vietnamese contract translation:*** If Vietnamese (bilingual) contract versions are made, it is essential that a precise and accurate Vietnamese translation is made. This is often overlooked or underestimated by foreign investors, who mostly rely on good quality standards when translations are made. However, even certified Vietnamese translation companies are often unable to translate legal terms accurately and precisely. For example, Vietnamese translations of English legal terms often confuse and/or do not clearly distinguish between their legal and commercial meaning of certain terms, even with relatively common terms such as e.g., "capital", "investment", "revenues" and "profits".
- ***Lack of definitions and inconsistency of contract terms:*** Specifically in cases where the Vietnamese party provides the first contract draft,

there are often no clear definitions of terms which may result in misunderstanding about their meaning. It is therefore important to introduce terms either in a separate paragraph, or where the term is first mentioned, a contract definition which in the following will only be used in capitalized form. Where annexes / appendixes are made, they must explicitly be made "integral part" of the contract and their use of defined terms must be consistent.

- *Disregard of Vietnamese legal terminology:* Vietnamese laws often have legal terms that deviate from internationally common terms. This is particularly true in the area of commercial and corporate law. For example, shareholders in a limited liability company are called "members" in Vietnam. And these "members" do not hold shares but "capital contributions" in the limited company. The meeting of shareholders in a limited company in Vietnam is called "Members' Council" meeting instead of shareholder meeting. Articles of association or bylaws are referred to in Vietnam as the "Company Charter" and there is a dogmatic difference between the investment and the charter capital in Vietnam. Therefore, English templates should be reviewed with regard to deviating terminology in Vietnam.
- *Missing and/or incomplete contract provisions:* Where the Vietnamese side provides contract drafts, there will often be a focus on certain (rather commercial) provisions such as payment and delivery terms, while other terms are either missing or incomplete. This is often true for e.g., liability-, confidentiality and data protection clauses, termination clauses, compliance clauses and entire agreement-, severability- and written-form clauses. In addition, some legal terms, concepts

and clauses are still not very well known in Vietnam, which may cause additional confusion on the Vietnamese side. This is for example the case with hold-harmless and indemnification clauses and tag-along/drag-along clauses in share purchase agreements.

- ***Insufficient dispute resolution clause:*** A good dispute resolution clause should generally include a two-step step approach with the first step being negotiation or mediation, however with a clear procedure including at least notification requirements and timelines for amicable resolution (e.g., 30 days). Only if negotiation fails, the dispute should be referred to in a second step to arbitration centres or Vietnamese courts. As mentioned above, referral to the VIAC rather than Vietnamese courts often makes sense, especially where simple commercial matters are concerned.

Summary: *If foreign templates are used for Vietnamese business transactions, local compliance with Vietnamese laws should be carefully checked. No template can fully anticipate all details and specifics of the case at hand. Don't rely on the quality of Vietnamese translations if bilingual contracts are made. Consider carefully the appropriate dispute resolution mechanism.*

2. Investment Licensing

2.1 Overview

2.1.1 Foreign and Domestic Investors

The amended Law on Investment No. 61/2020/QH14 (LOI) came into effect on 1st January 2021 and is supplemented by Decree 31/2021/ND-CP (Decree 31) effective since 26th March 2021. Art. 3 LOI generally defines as investor an "*organization or individual that carries out business investment activities*" in Vietnam. Auch investors include domestic investors, foreign investors and foreign-invested business entities as follows:

- A ***domestic investor*** means an individual holding Vietnamese nationality or a business entity whose members or shareholders are not foreign investors.
- A ***foreign investor*** means an individual holding a foreign nationality or an organization established under foreign laws and carrying our business investment activities in Vietnam.
- A ***foreign-invested business entity*** means a legal entity whose members or shareholders are foreign investors, with business entities only including entities established and operating in accordance with Vietnamese laws.

Under Art. 23 (1) LOI, certain foreign investors and foreign invested business entities, unlike domestic investors and business entities, must follow the investment registration procedures of the LOI when i) establishing a business entity, ii) making investments by contributing capital, purchasing shares or purchasing stakes of a business entity or iii) making investments under a business cooperation contract. In detail, the ***investment registration procedures of the LOI apply*** if:

- 50% or more of the investor's charter capital is held by (a) foreign investor(s) or the majority of partners are foreigners (if the business entity is a partnership).
- 50% or more of the investor's charter capital is held by one or more foreign invested business entity/entities.
- 50% or more of the investor's charter capital is held by one or more foreign investor(s) and one or more foreign invested business entity/entities.

According to Art. 37 LOI, investment projects of above defined investors (foreign investors) must first be issued an Investment Registration Certificate (IRC). Other investors only need to follow investment procedures also applied to Vietnamese domestic investors (if any). Therefore, unlike domestic investors, Foreign Investors are subject to two subsequent licensing procedures:

- Obtaining the IRC which approves the Foreign Investor's investment project in Vietnam, and then
- Obtaining the Enterprise Registration Certificate (ERC), with which the legal entity operating the foreign investment project is formally established (Foreign Invested Enterprise, FIE).

Accordingly, Foreign Investors carrying out their ***first investment project*** in Vietnam must not establish a FIE without a valid, approved investment project and the IRC issued prior to applying for the ERC which established the legal entity. If a Foreign Investor who has already licensed an investment project in Vietnam pursues a new investment project, procedures for executing such new, additional investment project shall be followed, however without necessarily having to establish a new, additional legal entity.

The same applies if a Foreign Investor wants to ***expand their existing investment project***: In this case, they can either use their existing FIE (and its ERC) or establish a new FIE (and then a new, additional ERC needs to be issued).

2.1.2 Investment Registration Certificate

The IRC application includes the foreign investor's "Investment Project Proposal" and the "Application for Investment Project Execution". The IRC application must be supported by the following legalized documents:

- The foreign investor's certificate of incorporation, articles of association, audited financial statements for the last two fiscal years and legal representatives' passport copies.
- The foreign investor's decision to establish a FIE in Vietnam and decision to appoint Authorized Representative(s), Legal Representative(s) and the General Director of the future FIE.
- Passport copies of Authorized Representative(s), Legal Representative(s) and the General Director of the future FIE.

- Memorandum of Understanding (MOU) regarding the lease of office space in Vietnam (the MOU will commit that the future FIE will then take over the lease after the ERC is issued).
- Commitment letter or bank statement to pay up the charter capital (sometimes asked for even though not legally required).

These supporting need to be "legalized" in the Foreign Investor's home country so that they can be used in Vietnam. The legalization procedure varies from country to country, but generally includes at least three steps:

Step 1: *The document must be authenticated by a competent notary public of the country where the documents were issued (usually within the district where the Foreign Investor is headquartered or residing).*

Step 2: *The notarized documents must then be certified by the competent diplomatic body of the country where the documents were issued. This can be the Ministry of Foreign Affairs, or in some countries the President of the Regional Court in which the notary public is located.*

Step 3: *The certified (pre-legalized) documents must then be legalized by the Vietnamese Embassy in the Foreign investor's home country.*

The legalized foreign documents must then be translated into Vietnamese and certified before they can be submitted to the licensing authorities in Vietnam. Even though the translation can be done abroad, if is preferable to have the legalized documents translated in Vietnam, because your advisors can then better double-check the translations provided by the Vietnamese certified translation company.

2.1.3 Licensing Timelines

According to Art. 38 (1) LOI, the deadline is within which the investment authority must grant or reject issuance of the IRC is 15 days from the date of receipt of the complete application documents. The additional ERC must be granted within three (3) working days. In practice, however, the licensing authorities will hardly ever meet those deadlines. Rather, they will often delay approvals with various arguments why the submitted application dossiers were not accurate or complete and therefore the legally prescribed timelines could not be kept or were not started in the first place. In this context direct or indirect demand for "acceleration payments" are sometimes made. In practice, foreign investors should calculate with at least twice the statutory timelines and also include the time required to obtain and legalize the documents required for the IRC and ERC applications.

2.1.4 Distribution and Retail

Additional licensing requirements: In some cases, in addition to IRC and ERC, additional licenses, permits and thus the participation of other agencies, authorities or ministries may be required. This is for example required in certain other business areas such as e.g., in education, banking and financial services, construction, hospitality, real estate and certain other limited investment areas.

Practically important for many investors is the area of retail- and distribution, in which, in addition to IRC and ERC, a distribution license (in Vietnam rather confusingly referred to as "business" / "trading" license and potentially additional "retail outlet establishment license(s)" must be obtained by the Department of Industry and Trade (DOIT).

Retail and distribution activities are governed by Decree No. 09/2018/ND-CP dated 15 January 2018 (Decree 9), which contains comprehensive regulations regarding *"activities directly related to sale of goods of foreign investors and foreign-invested business entities in Vietnam"*. According to Art. 5 of Decree 9, a business / trading license must generally be issued to a foreign-invested business entity to exercise retail and distribution rights, importation rights and wholesale distribution rights. Once issued, the validity of a business / trading license is five years. Note that in some cases, the DOIT requires the the approval of the Ministry of Industry and Trade's (MOIT) prior to license issuance, for example in the following cases: retail of rice, sugar, recorded items, books, newspapers and magazines which are distributed by the company in its retail outlets in forms of supermarkets, mini supermarkets or convenience stores.

Business / Trading license requirement: Art. 12 of Decree 9 requires – amongst others – that the foreign business must provide the following documentation to be issued a trading / business license:

- ***Business plan:*** business activities and methods of doing business; presentation of business plan and market development; labour need; evaluation of the implications and socio-economic effectiveness of the business plan;

- ***Financial plan:*** An income statement made on the basis of the last audited financial statement if the enterprise has been established in Vietnam for at least 1 year; representation of capital, sources of funds and fund-raising plans; enclosed with other financial documents;

- ***Tax documentation:*** A document justifying that the enterprise incurs no overdue tax issued by the tax authority; and
- ***Other documents:*** Copies of the ERC; certificate of registration for sale of goods and other related activities (if any).

Retail outlet establishment license (ROEL): Art. 22, 23 of Decree 9 contain the requirements for obtaining a ROEL. Note that each retail outlet must obtain a separate ROEL. Retail outlets which are (i) less than 500 sqm in size, or (ii) located in a shopping mall, and (iii) not classified as a convenience store/mini supermarket can be licensed without a so-called "Economic Needs Test" (ENT). However, all other (successive) retails outlets must complete the ENT process in order to be issued the ROEL

In particular, Art. 23 prescribes the criteria for the ENT which include amongst others i) the number of existing retail outlets in the relevant geographic market; ii) the impact of the retail outlet on the market stability and operating activities of other retail outlets and traditional markets in the relevant geographic market; iii) the impact of retail outlet on traffic density, environment hygiene, fire safety in the relevant geographic market and iv) the potential contribution of the retail outlet to the socio-economic development of the relevant geographic market, in particular: employment creation for domestic workers, potential contribution to the development and modernization of the retailing sector in the relevant geographic market, improvement of environment and living conditions of inhabitants in the relevant geographic market and potential and actual contribution to the state budget.

If a domestically owned company with retail outlet(s) in Vietnam is acquired by a FIE or foreign investor under the LOI, the FIE or foreign investor the must apply for both a business / trading license and ROELs for each retail outlet unless an exemption applies.

2.1.5 Investment Guarantees

General investment guarantee: Art. 10 LOI guarantees all investors that their lawful assets shall generally not be nationalized or confiscated by administrative measures. Only where an asset is bought or requisitioned by the State for reasons of national defense and security, national interests, state of emergency or natural disaster management, the investor shall be reimbursed or compensated in accordance with regulations of law on asset requisition and relevant regulations of law.

Profit- and asset repatriation guarantee: In addition, Art. 12. LOI guarantees the transfer of foreign investors' assets overseas if the foreign investor has fulfilled all tax/financial obligations. Those assets specifically include the foreign investors' i) investment capital and proceeds from liquidation of their investment, ii) income obtained from business investment activities and iii) money and other assets under their lawful ownership.

"Change of law" guarantee: Art. 13 LOI further provides investment guarantees for foreign investors in cases of changes in legislation: Where a new law provides more favourable investment incentives, investors are generally entitled to enjoy the new incentives for the remaining period of the incentive enjoyment of the project. Where a new law that provides less favourable investment incentives than those previously enjoyed by investor is promulgated, investors shall generally keep enjoying the current incentives for the remaining period of the incentive enjoyment of the project. Where an investor is no longer eligible for investment incentives, the following options exist: i) Deduction of the damage suffered by the investor from the investor's taxable income, ii) Adjustment of the objectives of the investment project or iii) Assisting the investor in remedying the damage.

2.2 Market Access Restrictions

2.2.1 General Restrictions

Under the LOI, both foreign and domestic investores may conduct freely all business activities in Vietnam, unless these business lines are either banned or conditional.

Banned business lines: Art. 6 LOI lists as banned business lines:

- *Trade in narcotic substances specified in Appendix I of the LOI.*
- *Trade in chemicals and minerals specified in Appendix II of the LOI.*
- *Trade in specimens of wild flora and fauna specified in Appendix 1 of the Convention on International Trade in Endangered Species of*

Wild Fauna and Flora; specimens of rare and/or endangered species of wild fauna and flora in Group I of Appendix III of the LOI.

- *Prostitution, human trafficking, trade in human tissues, corpses, human organs and human fetuses.*
- *Business activities pertaining to asexual human reproduction.*
- *Trade in firecrackers.*
- *Provision of debt collection services.*

Conditional Business Lines: Vietnam restricts or conditions investment into so-called "conditional sectors", which include certain sensitive sectors with impact on social order and/or state security; the education, healthcare and financial services sectors; the production, publication and distribution of cultural goods and the mining industry. Art. 7 (2) in connection with Appendix IV of the LOI lists 227 such conditional business lines. In addition, certain investments are limited to foreign investments with a particular threshold, such as investments in Vietnamese banks (30%) or investment in public enterprises (49%).

2.2.2 Additional Restrictions

For foreign investors, Art. 15-18 in connection with Appendix I of Decree 31 provide an additional "*list of business lines with prohibited and restricted market access*". Specifically, Art. 17 (1)-(2) of Decree 31 provide that Foreign Investors are only treated like domestic Vietnamese investors when investing in business lines which do not fall under the "***Negative List for Market***

Access", which is comprised of two sub-lists: A "***Prohibition List***" of business lines which Foreign Investors are not allowed to invest in, and a "***Market Entry List***" of business lines in which Foreign Investors must satisfy certain market entry conditions to invest in.

The "***Prohibition List***" lists 25 business lines prohibited for Foreign Investors because their foreign investment may harm Vietnam's national security and -defense, social order, community health, Vietnamese historical traditions, culture and customs and/or damage or destroy natural resources and the environment as follows:

1. *Trading goods and services on the list of goods and services on which monopoly is held by the State in the commercial sector.*
2. *Press activities and information gathering in any form.*
3. *Fishing.*
4. *Security and investigation services.*
5. *Judicial administration services, including services in judicial assessment, poste restante, property auction, notary and liquidation.*
6. *Overseas contracted employment agency services.*
7. *Investment in the construction of infrastructure of cemeteries and graveyards to transfer land use rights associated with such infrastructure.*
8. *Waste collection services directly from households.*
9. *Public opinion polling service (public opinion polling).*
10. *Blasting services.*

11. *Manufacture and trade in weapons, explosives and supporting tools.*
12. *Import and dismantling of used seagoing vessels.*
13. *Public postal services.*
14. *Goods transhipment business.*
15. *Temporary import for re-export business.*
16. *Exercise of the right to export, import, and distribution of goods on the list of goods for foreign investors, foreign-invested economic organizations are not allowed to exercise the right to export, import, distribute.*
17. *Collection, purchase and handling of public goods in armed forces units.*
18. *Trading in military materials or equipment and supplies for the people's armed forces, military weapons, technical equipment, ammunition and specialized vehicles used for the army and police; components, accessories, spare parts, supplies and specialized equipment and technology used for their production.*
19. *IPR representation services and industrial property assessment services.*
20. *Services of the establishment, operation, maintenance and maintenance of aids to navigation, water zones, water areas, public navigational channels and maritime routes; service of surveying water zones, water areas, public navigational channels and maritime routes serving maritime notices; services of surveying, constructing and publishing nautical charts for waters, seaports, navigational channels and maritime routes; building and publishing marine safety documents and publications.*

21. *Navigation services to ensure maritime safety in water areas, water areas and public navigational channels; marine electronic information service.*

22. *Inspection and certification services for means of transport (including systems, components, equipment, components of vehicles); inspection and issuance of certificates of technical safety and environmental protection for vehicles, specialized equipment, containers, and dangerous goods packaging equipment used in transportation; inspection services and issuance of certificates of technical safety and environmental protection for oil and gas exploration, exploitation and transportation means and equipment at sea; technical inspection service of occupational safety for machines and equipment with strict requirements on occupational safety installed on means of transport and means, exploration and exploitation equipment and oil and gas transportation at sea; fishing vessel registry services.*

23. *Natural forest investigation, assessment and exploitation services (including gathering wood and hunting, trapping rare wild animals, management of the sources genes for plants, livestock and microorganisms used in agriculture).*

24. *Researching or using genetic resources of new livestock breeds before being appraised and evaluated by the Ministry of Agriculture and Rural Development.*

25. *Tourism services, except international tourism services for international tourists to Vietnam.*

The ***"Market Entry List"*** lists 58 business lines in which Foreign Investors must satisfy certain market entry conditions and one "opening item" No. 59

which allows the issuance of "pilot mechanisms" on new business lines (rather than existing ones) Accordingly, if there is no pilot mechanism on a business line which falls within neither the Prohibition List nor the Market Entry List, Foreign Investors are equal to domestic investors in terms of market entry conditions. In detail:

1. *Production, distribution of cultural products, including visual recordings.*
2. *Production, distribution and broadcast of television programs and music, stage performance and motion picture works.*
3. *Supply of radio and television services.*
4. *Insurance, banking, securities brokerage, and other services related to insurance, banking, and securities.*
5. *Postal services, telecom services.*
6. *Advertising services.*
7. *Printing service, publication issuance services.*
8. *Measurement and mapping services.*
9. *FlyCam services.*
10. *Educational services.*
11. *Exploration, extraction, processing natural resources, minerals, oil/gas.*
12. *Hydropower, offshore wind power and nuclear energy.*
13. *Transport of goods and passengers by rail, road, air- and waterway.*
14. *Aquaculture cultivation or breeding.*

15. *Forestry and hunting.*
16. *Betting and casino business*
17. *Security guard services.*
18. *Construction, operation and management of river ports, sea- and airports.*
19. *Real estate business.*
20. *Legal services.*
21. *Veterinary services.*
22. *Goods sale and purchase activities and activities directly related to goods trading activities of foreign service providers in Vietnam.*
23. *Technical inspection and analysis services.*
24. *Travelling [tourism] services.*
25. *Health and social services.*
26. *Sports and entertainment services.*
27. *Paper production.*
28. *Manufacture of transport vehicles with more than 29 seats.*
29. *Development and operation of wet markets.*
30. *Commodity Exchange operations.*
31. *Domestic LCL collection services.*
32. *Auditing, accounting, bookkeeping and tax services.*
33. *Valuation sconsulting services on corporate valuation for equitization.*

34. *Services related to agriculture, forestry and fishery.*
35. *Aircraft manufacturing.*
36. *Manufacture of railway locomotives and wagons.*
37. *Trading tobacco products, tobacco raw materials, and specialized machinery and equipment for the tobacco industry.*
38. *Publishers' activities.*
39. *Ship building, and repair services.*
40. *Waste collection services, environmental observation services.*
41. *Commercial arbitration services, arbitration and mediation services.*
42. *Logistic services.*
43. *Coastal shipping.*
44. *Cultivation, production or processing of rare crops, breeding of rare wild animals, processing and handling of these animals or plants, including products thereof.*
45. *Production of construction materials.*
46. *Construction and related technical services.*
47. *Motorcycle assembly.*
48. *Services related to sports, art activities, performing arts, fashion shows, beauty and model contests, and other entertainment.*
49. *Air transport support services; airport ground technical and aircraft catering; navigation information services, aviation meteorological services.*

50. *Sea transport services; shipping tugboat [ship towing] services.*
51. *Services related to cultural heritage, copyright and related rights, photography, video recording, art exhibitions, festivals, libraries, museums.*
52. *Services related to tourism promotion.*
53. *Agent, recruitment, management for artists, athletes' services.*
54. *Family related services.*
55. *E-commerce activities.*
56. *cemetery business, cemetery services and funeral services.*
57. *Airborne seeding and chemical spraying services.*
58. *Maritime pilotage services.*
59. *Investment sector, business lines under the pilot mechanism of the National Assembly, The Standing Committee of the National Assembly, the Government, and the Prime Minister.*

In summary, according to Art. 17 of Decree 31, foreign investors are subject to the following additional market access restrictions:

- Foreign investors must not invest in the prohibited business lines specified in the ***Prohibition List*** (Section A, Appendix I of Decree 31/2021).
- For restricted business lines specified in the ***Market Entry List*** (Section B, Appendix I of Decree 31), foreign Investors shall fulfil the conditions that are published in accordance with Article 18 of Decree 31.

A foreign investor carrying out investment activities in different business lines specified in the Prohibition or Market Entry List must fulfil all market access conditions applied to those business lines. In business lines without above market access restrictions, foreign and domestic investors have equal market access, subjects to the applicable Vietnamese laws and regulations. If a ***new Vietnamese legislative document*** contains market access restrictions for foreign investors in the business lines without market-access commitment of Vietnam:

- Foreign investors to whom the conditions for market access mentioned have been applied ***before the new legislative document takes effect*** may carry on their investment activities under the said conditions.
- Foreign investors that carry out investment activities ***after the effective date of the new legislative document*** shall fulfil the market access conditions prescribed by such document.
- In case of ***establishment of a new business organization***, execution of a new investment project, receipt of an investment project, purchase of stakes/shares of another business organization under a contract or change to the objectives or business lines that is subject to fulfilment of market access conditions prescribed by the new legislative document, such conditions must be fulfilled. In this case, the competent authority shall not reconsider the conditions for market access in the business lines granted to the investor previously.

2.3 Investment Incentives

Tax incentives may apply for both new investment projects and expansion of existing investment projects, however restrictions may apply for the expansion of existing investment projects or investment projects resulting from certain acquisitions or restructuring transactions. Tax incentives only apply to the promoted investment activities and not for other, indirect or accidental income resulting from the investment activities (such as e.g., interest income, foreign currency income).

2.3.1 Types of Investment Incentives

Investment incentives include:

- Reduced corporate income tax (CIT) rates between 10% and 17% are granted for 15 or 10 years, starting with the beginning revenue generation from the tax-funded activities. The duration of the application of the preferred tax rate may be extended in certain cases. The preferential rate of 15% applies in certain cases for the entire project period. Certain sectors (e.g., education, health) also enjoy the 10% preferential tax rate throughout the project life.

- Tax exemption means a time period in which the investment project is completely exempted from CIT, starting from the first financial year in which the company generates a profit.

- Tax reduction refers to the subsequent period of time to the period of tax exemption, in which a 50% reduction is granted to the relevant CIT rate. If the company does not generate a profit within three years, the tax exemption or tax reduction begins in each case from the fourth financial year.
- Exemption from import duties may apply for certain investment projects with special investment incentives or those in socio-economically difficult areas if the imported goods are part of the fixed assets of the investment project in Vietnam.
- Exemption from and reduction of land levy and land rents may be granted based on the nature of the investment project.
- Accelerated depreciation, increasing the deductible expenses upon calculation of taxable income.

2.3.2 Special Investment Incentives

Projects and entities eligible for investment incentives:

- Investment projects, outside the mining sector or such projects whose products are subject to special sales tax, with an investment volume of 6,000 billion VND or more (within three years from licensing), if they meet at least one of the following criteria: Revenue of at least 10,000 billion VND per year, starting with the fourth year of business, or more than 3,000 employees at the latest in the fourth year of business operations.

- Investment projects on establishment or expansion of innovation- or research and development centres with a total investment capital of 3,000 billion VND or more and which disburses at least 1,000 billion VND within a period of three years from the date of being granted the IRC or Investment Policy Approval or national innovation centres established under the decision of the Prime Minister.
- Investment projects in industries and trades eligible for special investment incentives with an investment capital of at least 30,000 billion VND and which disburses at least 10,000 billion VND within a period of three years from the date of being granted the IRC or Investment Policy Approval.
- Investment projects with an investment volume of at least 12,000 billion VND distributed within five years of licensing, except for mining projects or projects whose products are the subject to special sales tax.
- Social housing construction projects; investment projects located in rural areas and employing at least 500 employees, investment projects that employ persons with disabilities in accordance with the laws on persons with disabilities.
- High-technology enterprises, science and technology enterprises and science and technology organizations, projects involving transfer of technologies on the "list of technologies the transfer of which is encouraged" in accordance with the Law

on Technology Transfer, science and technology enterprise incubators prescribed by the Law on High Technologies and Law on Science and Technology, enterprises manufacturing and providing technologies, equipment, products and services aiming at meeting environment protection requirements prescribed by the Law on Environment Protection.

- Business investment in small and medium-sized enterprises (SMEs) product distribution chains eligible for investment incentives or in a network of intermediaries that distribute products of such SMEs to consumers and meet the following conditions: At least 80% of enterprises joining the chain are SMEs, there are at least 10 places for distribution of goods to consumers and at least 50% of revenue of the chain are generated by SMEs joining the chain.
- Investment in SME incubators, technical establishments supporting SMEs, co-working spaces supporting start-up SMEs eligible for investment incentives (those established in line with the laws on provision of assistance for SMEs).
- Start-up investment projects on manufacturing of products created from inventions, utility solutions, industrial designs, semiconductor integrated circuits layout-designs, computer software, applications on mobile phones, cloud computing, production of new livestock breed or line, new plant varieties, new aquatic breeds, new forest tree cultivars, technological advances which have been granted IPR or copyright protection.

- Projects on manufacturing of products obtained from projects on trial production, sample products and technology completion, manufacturing of products given awards at (national) start-up competitions, scientific and technological awards.

Business activities eligible for investment incentives:

- High-tech activities, high-tech ancillary products, research, manufacturing and development of from science and technology products in line with the law on science and technology.
- Manufacturing of new, clean and renewable energies, manufacturing of products with an added value of 30% or more and energy-saving products.
- Manufacturing of key electronics, mechanical products, agricultural machinery, automobiles and parts, shipbuilding.
- Manufacturing of products on the list of prioritized supporting products.
- Manufacturing of IT and software products, digital contents.
- Breeding, growing and processing of agriculture products, forestry products, aquaculture products, afforestation and forest protection, salt production, fishing and fishing logistics services, production of plant varieties, animal breeds and biotechnology products.
- Collection, treatment, recycling or re-use of waste.

- Investment in development, operation, management of infrastructural works; public transportation in urban areas.
- Pre-school, higher, general and vocational education.
- Medical examination and treatment; manufacturing of medicinal products and medicinal materials, storage of medicinal products; scientific research into preparation technology and biotechnology serving creation of new medicinal products; manufacturing of medical equipment.
- Sports facilities for disabled or professional athletes.
- Protection and promotion of value of cultural heritage.
- Investment in geriatric and centres for elderly, mental health centres, treatment for agent orange patient, the disabled, orphans and street children.
- Investment in people's credit funds, microfinance institutions.
- Manufacturing of goods and provision of services for creating or participating in value chains and industrial clusters.

Areas eligible for investment incentives:

- Disadvantaged areas and extremely disadvantaged areas.
- Industrial parks; export-, hi-tech- and economic zones.

2.4 Investment Policy Approval

As a general rule, investment approval is granted by ***IRC issuance*** by either the provincial Department of Planning and Investment (DPI) or the Management Boards of industrial parks, export-processing zones, hi-tech zones and economic zones (if the investment project is executed in such industrial park, export-processing zone, hi-tech or economic zone). However, for below selected special investment projects, an ***Investment Policy Approval (IPA)*** is required in addition to the IRC. In these cases, the licensing authority depends on the type and scale of the investment project.

2.4.1 Large-Scale Investment Projects

The ***National Assembly*** approves the following investment projects:

1. Investment projects that exert great effects or potentially serious effects on the environment, including nuclear power plants, projects that require repurposing of special-use forests, headwater protection forests or border protection forests of at least 50 hectares; of sand-fixing and windbreak coastal forests or protection forests for wave prevention of at least 500 hectares or production forests of at least 1,000 hectares.

2. Investment projects that require repurposing of land meant for wet rice cultivation during with two or more crops of at least 500 hectares.

3. Investment projects that require relocation of 20,000 people or more in mountainous areas or 50,000 people or more in other areas.

4. Investment projects that require application of a special mechanism or policy that needs National Assembly approval.

2.4.2 Medium-Scale Investment Projects

Except for investment projects to be approved by the National Assembly, the ***Prime Minister*** approves the following investment projects:

i) Investment projects regardless of capital sources:

- Investment projects that require relocation of 10,000 people in mountainous areas or over 20,000 people in other areas.
- Investment projects on construction of airports and aerodromes, runways of airports and aerodromes, international passenger terminals, cargo terminals of airports and aerodromes with a capacity of at least one million tonnes per year.
- New investment projects on passenger air transport business.
- Investment projects on construction of ports and wharves of special seaports, ports and wharves in which investment is at least VND 2,300 billion within the category of class I seaports.
- Investment projects on petroleum processing.

- Investment projects which involve betting and casino services, excluding business in prize-winning electronic games for foreigners.
- Projects on construction of residential housing (for sale, lease or lease purchase) and urban areas that use at least 50 hectares of land or less than 50 hectares of land but with a population of at least 15,000 people in an urban area; or investment projects that use at least 100 hectares of land or less than 100 hectares of land but with a population of at least 10,000 people in a non-urban area; or investment projects regardless of the area of land used or population within the safety perimeter of relics recognized by the competent authority as the national and special national relics.
- Investment projects on construction and operation of infrastructure in industrial zones and export processing zones.

ii) Investment projects of Foreign Investors in the following fields: provision of telecommunications services with network infrastructure, afforestation, publication and press.

iii) Investment projects which at the same time fall within the power of at least two provincial People's Committees to grant approval for investment guidelines.

iv) Other investment projects subject to approval for their investment guidelines or subject to issuance of decisions on investment guidelines by the Prime Minister as prescribed by law.

2.4.3 Small-Scale Investment Projects

The remaining special "small-scale" investment projects which are not under the approval authority of the National Assembly or the Prime Minister are approved by the provincial ***People's Committees***:

i) Investment projects that request the State to allocate or lease out land without auction or bidding for or receipt of land use rights, and investment projects that request permission to repurpose land, except for cases of land allocation, land lease or permission for land repurposing by family households or individuals not subject to the written approval by the provincial People's Committee as prescribed in the law on land.

ii) Projects on construction of residential housing (for sale, lease or lease purchase) and urban areas that use at least 50 hectares of land or less than 50 hectares of land but with a population of at least 15,000 people in an urban area; or that use at least 100 hectares of land or less than 100 hectares of land but with a population of at least 10,000 people in a non-urban area; or investment projects regardless of the area of land used or population within a restricted development area or within an historic inner area (determined in accordance with urban area planning projects) of a special urban area.

iii) Investment projects on construction and operation of golf courses.

iv) Investment projects of foreign investors and foreign-invested business entities executed on islands or in border or coastal communes, in other areas affecting national defense and security.

2.4.4 Industrial and Economic Zones

Hundreds of industrial and economic zones exist in Vietnam, their main benefits being their good infrastructure, legal certainty of land titles and the reliability of tax benefits.

There are three different types as follows:

- ***Industrial Zones (IZs):*** The IZs specialize in the production of various industrial goods. The 150 IZs in operation or construction occupy a total area of about 100,000 hectares within Vietnam. The IZs in operation often have an occupancy rate of over 75%, with some popular IZs often fully occupied.
- ***High-Tech Zones (HTZs):*** HTZs are multifunctional zones which companies can use to produce high-tech goods, conduct research and development or train personnel, which can be later be employed in the HTZs. Foreign Investor's interest in HTZs has recently been lower, mainly because of the benefits and incentives offered are very similar to those offered in IZs, and only small clusters for science and technology having arisen in and around the existing HTZs.
- ***Economic Zones (EZs):*** The EZs are defined as certain geographical areas where investment privileges are granted just like in the IZs. As EZs are mostly located in structurally weak regions, foreign investors are usually offered better incentives as in the IZs, mostly with regards to favourable rates for land use rights. Currently there are around 20 EZs in Vietnam.

2.5 Foreign Investors' Land Use Rights

2.5.1 Types and Duration

Land Use Rights (LURs) are governed by the Vietnamese Land Law No. 45/2013/QH13 (Land Law). Art. 4 Land Law provides that the *"Land belongs to the entire people with the State acting as the owner's representative and uniformly managing land. The State shall grant land use rights to land users in accordance with this Law."* Accordingly, the Land Law only recognizes land "ownership" in form of LURs. While the Land Use Right Certificate ("LURC") is similar to a title deed in many countries, it is technically speaking only a certificate of "ownership" of the LUR.

Art. 5 No. 7 Land Law includes as potential land users *"Foreign-invested enterprises, including 100% foreign-invested enterprises, joint-venture enterprises, Vietnamese enterprises in which foreign investors purchase shares, merge or acquire in accordance with investment law."* Art. 5 Land Law stipulates that a number of "land users" may obtain LURs as follows:

- ***Allocation of LURs:*** In such case, the LUR will be granted on a long-term basis, i.e., without a specific duration of use. However, LURs will mostly be allocated to Vietnamese citizens or organizations for limited purposes. Accordingly, allocation most closely resembles "real" ownership. Allocated land must be paid for in a lump-sum payment.
- ***Recognition of LURs:*** In such case, the LUR will be first granted for the stable land use which does not originate from allocation

or lease. As the state can "recognize" LURs for national entities only, this method only plays a practical role in cases where LURs are recognized for a Vietnamese JV partner.

- ***"Acquisition" of LURs:*** In such case, the LUR will be granted for a specific duration of time against the payment of a usage-fee. Accordingly, even where sometimes referred to as "ownership", the granting of the LUR by acquisition mostly resembles a long-term lease contract with the lease paid upfront.

2.5.2 LURs in Foreign Investment Projects

Foreign investors may obtain LURs for their investment project by:

- Acquiring the LUR from the state by entering into a lease-agreement and paying the LUR fee annually or in one upfront lump-sum payment.
- Acquiring an existing investment project from other investors, and taking-over the project's current lease-agreement.
- Entering into a Joint Venture ("JV") with a Vietnamese JV partner who obtains the LUR and contributes it to the JV.
- Receiving a land allocation from the state, with payment of the land use fee for specific investment projects, e.g., on the construction of houses for sale or a combination of sale and lease.

A lot of cases in which foreign investors "acquire" land relate to JVs between Foreign Investors and a domestic investor who contributes the

LUR into the JV in kind, valued at its current market price. The reason being that Foreign Investors in most cases cannot legally obtain that land without jointly investing with the Vietnamese LUR owner (and JV partner). In addition, sometimes the relevant land is located in attractive investment areas and has been in use by local entities (often state-owned enterprises) who would neither sell, lease or allocate the LUR to the Foreign Investor alone, but only to a Vietnamese party.

According to Art. 126 (2) Land Law, the term for land allocation or land lease shall be considered and decided on the basis of the investment projects or applications for land allocation or land lease but must not exceed 50 years. For certain large investment projects with slow recovery of capital, projects in areas with difficult or especially difficult socio-economic conditions which require a longer term, the term of land allocation or land lease must not exceed 70 years.

2.5.3 Payment of Land Lease Fee

Foreign Investors who acquire LURs from the Government by entering into a LUR lease agreement may pay rent either on an annual basis or as a lump-sum payment:

Annual rental payment: Foreign investors paying annually may use the land for the approved investment purposes only, and is only allowed to transfer, sub-lease or mortgage the assets attached to the land, but not the LUR itself. If paid annually, the rental price is generally at market price (often between 1-3% of the land value is applied, and a lower rate of 0.5-1% may be applied for "low-yield" or agricultural land).

Upfront payment for entire lease term: Foreign Investors paying upfront for the entire lease term are entitled to transfer both the LUR and the assets attached to the land, subleasing land and assets attached to the land, contributing the LUR and assets attached to the land as capital to JVs, mortgaging or guaranteeing the LUR to credit institutions in Vietnam.

2.6 Foreign Investment Accounts

Requirement to open Foreign Investor's investment accounts: Circular No. 06/2019/TT-NHNN (Circular 6) provides guidance on foreign exchange management for foreign direct investment in Vietnam, including capital contributions, opening and use of foreign currency and VND direct investment accounts as well as the transfer of capital and profits and legal revenues to foreign countries. Circular 6, Art. 4 (3) provides that Foreign Investors' "capital contributions" for an investment project must be transferred to the Foreign Investor's "direct investment account" (DIA). DIAs are defined as "*foreign currency or Vietnamese Dong demand accounts opened by FDI enterprises and foreign investors at authorized banks to perform transactions regarding the foreign direct investment in Vietnam.*"

A DIA must generally be opened in the name of the FIE. Only exceptionally, the DIA will be opened in the name of the foreign investor if no FIE is established, such as in a business cooperation contract (BCC) or in public-private partnership contracts (PPP contracts). Practically, Foreign Investors shall open their foreign currency DIA at one licensed bank in Vietnam in order to receive and make payments in that foreign currency during their investment project in Vietnam. Generally, only one foreign currency DIA shall be opened, however in case of investing in VND, a foreign investor may open one Vietnamese Dong DIA at the same bank where the foreign currency DIA is opened in order to receive and make payment in VND during the term of the Foreign Investor's investment project.

Documents to be provided to open a DIA can be the IRC or "Establishment and Operation Certificate, the M&A approval or a BCC / PPP contract signed with an authorized state body or any other documents showing that the Foreign Investor's project is permitted.

Transfers required to be made through the DIA: Foreign investors' overseas transfers of foreign currency relating to their investment project must be made through the DIA. Such transfers include the following:

- Capital contributions to the FIE or transfers relating to Foreign Investors' BCCs or PPP projects.
- Transfers to increase or decrease the FIE's charter capital.
- Transfers relating to foreign currency loans to the FIE.
- Payment for the transfer of investment capital / projects.
- Overseas transfers of capital, lawful revenues and profits from the FIEs foreign currency DIA, including Foreign Investor's implementing BBCs or PPP projects.
- Termination of investment projects and transfer of investment and charter capital overseas.

Foreign investors who do not make required payments through a DIA risk being subject to a capital gains tax amounting to 20 percent.

Transfer of capital for the pre-investment stage: Before obtaining the IRC, the "Establishment and Operation Certificate" or before signing BCCs and PPP contracts, Foreign Investors are allowed to transfer their investments from overseas or from their accounts in foreign currencies or Vietnamese Dong opened at authorized banks to pay for legal expenditures in the pre-investment stage in Vietnam.

Closing of DIAs & shifting to "indirect investment accounts": FIE's shall close their DIAs where the foreign ownership ratio in the FIE falls below the threshold to qualify as a foreign investor as a result of i) the foreign investor transferring capital contributions or shares, ii) the FIE issuing additional capital contributions / shares in charter capital increases or iii) the FIE is becoming a publicly listed company. FIE's shall also close their DIAs where the FIE is dissolved the investment project is terminated or a transfer of the ownership of the investment project occurs, or where such transfer results in the change of the FIE's legal status. In these cases, foreign investors have the right to use their foreign currency and VND accounts opened at authorized banks to purchase foreign currency and transfer their direct investments and lawful revenues overseas in foreign currency.

In some of the above cases where foreign investors close their DIA, they may then be required to open an "Indirect Investment Account" (IIA) to continue their now indirect investment activities in Vietnam. Foreign indirect investment means that foreign investors make an investment into

Vietnam by buying securities, capital and purchase of shares, and investment funds without direct participation in the management of investment activities. Transaction related to indirect investments must be done through an IIA at a licensed bank in VND. Profits that are obtained from indirect investment activities must also be remitted by using the IIA.

Profit Repatriation: Profits must be deposited into the above DIA or IIA. Only once all tax- and other obligations relating to profits and distributions have been met, profits and proceeds of investments may then be converted back into foreign currency and remitted abroad. Profits may only be transferred abroad once annually at the end of each fiscal year.

2.7 Practical Tips

- ***Check if restrictions or conditions apply for your investment project:*** It is essential for potential investors to carefully examine if and under which conditions their investment project can be licensed in Vietnam. Sometimes, foreign ownership restrictions exist or there must be at least one Vietnamese shareholder to be active in certain business lines.

- ***Check local licensing differences:*** While in some cities or provinces, an "investor-friendly" approach will be taken, other cities or provinces may be less supportive. Therefore, prior to applying for the approval of an investment project, it is advisable to informally clarify with the licensing authority, which procedures and peculiarities should be observed, which documents should be submitted in which form and how specific procedural rules are interpreted by the licensing body in practice.

- ***Invest in industrial or economic zones where possible:*** Industrial and economic zones are often preferable to "greenfield" investments, as they mostly have good infrastructure, legal certainty of land titles and reliability of tax benefits. The management of the IZs or EZs will mostly be keen on supporting.
- ***Check available tax- and other investment incentives:*** The granting of certain investment incentives, primarily tax incentives, will often be essential for investment decision for Vietnam (as opposed to other countries in the region). Therefore, a thorough check of tax incentives available should be conducted.
- ***Be aware of investment capitalization requirements:*** Investment licensing authorities require IRC applicants to state in their investment proposal an investment capital for their investment project. Even though in most areas, no legal thresholds exist, the licensing authority will validate if the stated amount is in their view sufficient to seriously implement the project. As a rule of thumb, they will usually consider whether the stated investment capital is sufficient to start and sustain the investment project for at least one year. Accordingly, while 25K USD may be sufficient investment capital for a consulting business, it cannot be sufficient to set up a manufacturing facility with

hundreds of workers or a warehouse. In those cases, amounts starting from 200K USD will be more likely.

- ***Have complete, accurate and legalized documentation:*** The applications for obtaining the IRC and ERC contain a large number of supporting documents that must be obtained in the foreign investors' home countries. Some of those documents, such as certain resolutions and decisions, should be prepared by lawyers familiar with Vietnamese legal terminology.
- ***Consistently use your DIA for all investment-related transactions:*** Foreign investors' overseas transfers of foreign currency relating to their investment project must be made through the DIA. If not, this can not only result in difficulties with regards to repatriation of profits and proceeds, but also in taxation or non-deductibility of the transfers made into Vietnam. The same is true with regards to private loans that are made to supplement investment financing or other investment purposes.

***

Summary:

Carefully plan your investment project in Vietnam prior to execution. Important aspects include feasibility of the project in terms of investment location-, permitting and financing. Always prefer setting-up a 100% foreign-owned subsidiary to a joint venture with a Vietnamese counterpart unless absolutely necessary. Don't try to circumvent the requirements of the LOI by engaging a Vietnamese proxy.

3. Company Formation

3.1 Overview

The Limited Liability Company (LLC) is by far the most popular company form for Foreign Invested Enterprises (FIEs) and therefore chosen by the majority of foreign Investors when investing in Vietnam. While the Joint Stock Company (JSC, based on shares) is another viable option, it is rarely because of its more complicated administration and corporate governance. It may, however, be suitable in case of larger capital needs from the outset and subsequently if foreign investors want to access the domestic capital markets for further funding in the future. It is also useful if funding and voting shall be separated for example by issuing preferential shares alongside ordinary shares. In practice, however, foreign investors mostly take a two-step approach and open a LLC first before they would then contemplate converting it into a JSC.

3.1.1 Legal Representatives

Both LLC and JSC must have at least one so-called "Legal Representative" (LR) and at least one LR must reside in Vietnam. The LOE defines the LR as the *"individual who represents the enterprise to exercise the rights and perform the obligations arising from transactions of the enterprise, and represents the enterprise in the capacity as plaintiff, respondent or person with related interests and obligations before the arbitration or court, and other rights and obligations as prescribed by law."* If there is more than one LR, the FIE's company charter needs to precisely specify the number, managerial titles and rights and obligations of the FIE's LR(s). LRs have the obligation to:

- Exercise vested rights and perform assigned obligations in an honest, prudent and best manner in order to protect the lawful interests of the enterprise.
- Be faithful to the interests of the enterprise; not to use business information, know-how and opportunities of the enterprise; not to abuse their title, position and assets of the enterprise for personal purposes or for the interests of others.
- Notify the enterprise in a timely, sufficient and accurate manner about him/her and his/her affiliated persons owning or having controlling shares or contributed capital amounts in, other enterprises.

The LOE strictly distinguishes between the FIE's LR(s) and its General Director (GD) who will regularly be employed by the company.

Strict distinction between GD and LR: *Even though the GD will, for practical reasons, usually also be appointed as a LR, it is not legally required that the company's GD also be its LR. On the contrary, the company may appoint a LR without the LR being the GD or having any other corporate function in the company (even though this is rather uncommon). This is important, as the company's LR - other than the GD - is personally liable under the LOE for any damage caused to the enterprise by breaches of his/her obligations, even if the LR was unaware of any breaches by the acting GD.*

Foreign expatriate employees requested or instructed by their overseas employers to act as the GD and LR of the employer's FIE abroad should therefore request their overseas employers to indemnify and hold them harmless against any personal liability resulting from their appointment as the FIE's LR. This is even more urgent if they are requested to act as the GD or LR of additional or several subsidiaries abroad. Ideally, employees insist on a comprehensive indemnification agreement with their employer.

A minimal indemnification clause could be the following: *The Employer shall indemnify and hold Indemnitee harmless in respect of all claims and losses arising out of, or in connection with, the actual or purported exercise of, or failure to exercise, any of the Indemnitee's powers, duties or responsibilities as the General Director or Legal Representative.*

3.1.2 The Company Charter

The FIE's company charter, also known as articles of association, is its constitutional corporate governance document. It must contain at least the:

- FIE's name, headquarters, branches and representative offices.
- The FIE's business lines, its investment / charter capital (for JSCs the number, type and face value of shares).
- FIE's organizational structure (management model).
- Full names, mailing address, nationality of each member (for LLCs) or the founding shareholders (for JSCs) as well as the

charter capital held by each member (for LLCs) or quantity of shares, types of shares and value of each type held by founding shareholders (for JSCs).

- Rights and obligations of the members (for LLCs) or shareholders (for JSCs).
- Number, titles, rights and obligations of the FIE's LRs.
- Procedure for ratifying the FIE's decisions.
- Rules for settlement of internal disputes.
- Basis and method to determine executive salaries and bonuses.
- Cases in which members or shareholders may request the company to repurchase their capital contributions or shares.
- Rules and procedures for the distribution of profits and losses after each fiscal year.
- Cases, rules and procedures for the dissolution and liquidation of the company's assets.
- Procedures for amending the company charter.

3.1.3 Enterprise Registration Certificate

The establishment of legal entities in Vietnam is governed by the Law on Enterprises No. 59/2020/QH14 (LOE). After IRC issuance, foreign investors must in addition apply for the "Enterprise Registration Certificate" (ERC), with which the Vietnamese company comes into legal existence.

The following information must be provided in the enterprise registration application form:

1. The enterprise's name (Vietnamese, English and abbreviated form), headquarters, phone- and fax number and email address;
2. The enterprise's investment / charter capital; its business lines and expected number of employees;
3. Name, signature, mailing address and nationality of the enterprise's future legal representative(s);
4. The enterprise's tax registration information.

The ERC application form must be supplemented by the follow documentation in notarized /legalized (foreign documents) form:

- The FIE's IRC,
- The FIE's draft company charter / articles of association,
- The FIE's list of company members (LLC) or founding shareholders (JSC) / list of shareholders that are foreign investors,
- The FIE's list of members or shareholders (for legal entities) or passport copy for individual members / shareholders,
- Other documentation as the case may be.

While the LOE itself requires no minimum capitalization, the investment licensing authorities will require a minimum charter capital in line with the investment capital that was basis for the the prior IRC application and issuance.

In principle, foreign investors may contribute their capital in cash or in kind (e.g., through LURs, IPRs, technology, know-how etc). However, foreign investors' contributions in kind are unusual, mostly because of time delays caused by validating and evidencing that the value of the contribution in kind matches the stated investment and charter capital amount. Therefore, foreign investors will in most cases simply contribute their committed investment and charter capital in cash by transferring it to the company's DIA after the company's ERC has formally been established.

Payment of the investment- / charter capital to the FIE's bank account: *The charter capital of the LLC must be transferred in VND to the FIE's bank account within 90 days from the issuance of the ERC. The amount to be transferred must correspond exactly to the charter capital as stated in the ERC. In practice, it will be transferred in foreign currency to the FIE's DIA and then converted by the Vietnamese bank into VND. The non-fulfilment of this obligation can have serious consequences, in a worts case the revocation of the IRC/ERC.*

3.1.4 Post-licensing Procedures

After the ERC is issued and the FIE established, the following post-licensing procedures are required to make the FIE operational:

- Publication of the company establishment on the National Enterprise Registration Portal.

- Obtaining the company seal: The FIE can freely decide on the number, form and content of the seal/stamp. The seal specimen must be submitted to the business registration authorities for acknowledgement and public announcement.
- Paying the "business license tax" amounting to 2 million VND (equaling 85 USD) forFIEs with less than 10 billion VND charter capital, payable within 30 days after ERC issuance.
- Open (a) company bank account(s) in VND and foreign currency at a Vietnamese licensed bank or financial institution and register the bank account(s) with the tax department.
- Selecting an E-invoice service provider and register E-invoices with the tax authorities; purchase token keys for online tax lodgements from a licensed service provider.
- Initial tax registration for tax lodgements and payments via E-tax payment must be undertaken within 10 working days from ERC issuance.
- Appointing a company employee or licensed service provider as a the company's chief accountant, except where such appointment is not required (e.g., less than 10 employees).
- Register the FIE with labour authorities and insurance departments to lawfully hire employees.

3.2 Limited Liability Company

The LLC can be established either as a 100% foreign-owned subsidiary or with both domestic and foreign participation. While the latter case is often referred to as "Joint Venture" (JV), the JV does not exist as a separate company form. In practice, most foreign investors prefer the establishment of a 100% foreign-owned subsidiary over a JV whenever possible. Both legal entities and individuals may become "shareholders" of an LLC. The LLC can have a up to a maximum of 50 so-called "members" (i.e. "shareholders"). Depending on the number of members, the LOE distinguishes between a "Single Member Limited Liability Company" (SLLC) and a "Multiple Member Limited Liability Company" (MLLC). For both forms, liability is limited to the amount of the members' capital contribution.

3.2.1 Organizational Structures

SLLC with individual ownership: Must only have a Company President (President) and a GD. President may work as the GD concurrently or hire another person to work as the GD. The rights and obligations of the GD are provided in the company charter and the GD's employment contract.

SLLC with institutional ownership: Can choose between two organizational models with the following bodies: i) Members' Council (MC), GD and Supervisor, or ii) Chairman/President, GD and Supervisor. While the first model is needed to implement a "four-eye"-principle in the company, the second model simplifies the decision-making and efficiency as only the Chairman decides.

MLLC: Must have a MC, the Chairperson of the MC and a GD. In addition, MLLCs with 11 or more members must set up a Supervisory Board. If the MLLC has less than 11 members, installing a Supervisory Board is still possible but not required by law.

3.2.2 Corporate Governance:

The MC (SLLC and MLLC): Is composed of the totality of members and the highest decision-making body of the company. The MC comprises at least two members with terms not exceeding five years. The members are appointed or relieved by the investor / company owner. The rights and obligations of the MC are detailed in the company charter. The MC decides on strategic matters, while the GD decides on the company's day-to-day business. Specifically, the MC shall adopt resolutions about the following:

- Development strategies, the company's annual business plan, increase or reduction of the charter capital, investment projects of the company, solutions for market development, marketing and technology transfer.
- Approval of loan agreements and contracts for sale of assets valued at 50 or more percent of the total value of assets of the company as per the last financial statements.
- Appointment, relieving of duty, removal of the Chairperson, GD, chief accountant and other management personnel.
- Wages, bonus and other benefits for the Chairperson, the GD, chief accountant and other management personnel.

- Approval of the annual financial statements and plans for use and distribution of profits or plans for dealing with losses.
- Establishment of subsidiaries and branches.
- Amendments and supplements to the company charter.
- Adoption of annual financial statements.
- Reorganization, dissolution or request of insolvency.

For a ***quorum to be present*** at the first meeting of the MC, members representing 65% of the charter capital must be present. If there is no quorum at the first meeting, a second meeting must be held within 15 days. In the second meeting, a quorum is reached if 50% of the charter capital is present. If there is still no quorum, a third meeting is held within 10 working days at which there is no minimum attendance to obtain a quorum.

A ***resolution is adopted*** (after a quorum is reached) if it is approved by the number of votes representing at least 65 percent of the total contributed capital amount of the attending members. However, 75 percent of the votes are needed for decisions relating to the sale of assets valued at 50 or more percent of the total value of assets recorded in the company's latest financial statements and the liquidation of the company.

Deviations from resolution adoption thresholds: *The FIE's company charter may deviate from the "default" resolution thresholds above. For example, the company charter may provide for simple majority decisions adopted with 51% of the votes for "standard" decisions and 65% of the votes for "grave" decisions.*

Chairperson of the MC (MLLC and SLLC): The MC shall elect a member to be its Chairperson. While the term of the Chairperson of the MC must not exceed 5 years, the Chairperson may be re-elected for an unlimited number of terms. The Chairperson of the MC may concurrently work as the company's GD. The Chairperson has, amongst others, has the rights and obligations to:

- Prepare the MC's working programs and plans as well as the agenda and documents for meetings of the MC and for collecting Members' opinions.
- To convene and preside over meetings of the MC or to organize the collection of opinions of members and to sign MC resolutions and meeting minutes.
- To supervise, or to organize the supervision of, the implementation of resolutions of the MC.

President (SLLC only): The President of a SLLC shall be appointed by the company owner and exercise the rights of the company owner, except the rights and obligations of the GD.

General Director (MLLC and SLLC): The MC or the President (SLLC) appoints/hires the GD for a term not exceeding 5 years each to manage day-to-day business operations of the company. The Chairperson of the MC, another member of the MC or the President (SLLC) may concurrently act as the GD. The GD's rights and obligations include:

- To decide on all matters related to the day-to-day business operations of the company.

- To organize the implementation of decisions of the MC or the President (SLLC) and to organize the implementation of business plans and investment plans.
- To appoint, relieve of duty and remove from office managers and other staff in the company, except those falling within the competence of the MC or the President (SLLC).
- To sign contracts, except cases falling within the competence of the MC or the President (SLLC).
- To submit annual financial statements to the MC or the President (SLLC) for approval and to make recommendations on the use of profits or handling of losses.

Supervisors (only SSLC with institutional ownership): The company owner shall appoint at least one Supervisor for a term not exceeding 5 years. A supervisor has the following rights and obligations:

- To check the lawfulness, honesty and prudence of the company's management and key personnel in managing and running the business of the company.
- to evaluate financial statements, reports on business situations, reports on assessment of management work and other reports before submitting them to the company owner or relevant state agencies, submit evaluation reports to the company owner and to examine any other company documents.

3.3 Joint Stock Company

3.3.1 Overview

The JSC is an enterprise in which the charter capital is divided into equal portions called shares. Shareholders of the JSC may be organizations or individuals. The minimum number of shareholders when establishing a JSC is three. Shareholders are liable only with the amount of share capital contributed to the enterprise (or the share price paid). Shareholders may freely assign their shares to other persons, except where there are contractual holding obligations or other specific legal requirements such as pre-emptive rights. A JSC must have ordinary shares and may issue preference shares. Ordinary shares have one vote each, while perefernce shares shall not have voting rights. Ordinary shareholders have the following rights:

- To attend and express their opinions at the General Meeting of Shareholders (GMS) and to exercise their voting right with each ordinary share carrying one vote.
- To receive dividends as decided by the GMS.
- Priority in purchasing new shares offered for sale in proportion to the number of ordinary shares the shareholder holds.
- To freely transfer their shares, except where contractual restrictions such as a shareholders' agreement or other legal restrictions exist.

- To examine / extract information in the shareholders' registry and to request modification of incorrect information therein.
- To examine, extract or copy the company charter, the meetings of the GMS and the resolutions of the GMS Shareholders.
- Upon dissolution or insolvency of the company, to receive part of the residual assets in proportion to their number of shares.

A shareholder (group) holding at least 10 percent of the totally issued ordinary shares for a consecutive period of at least six months, or holding a smaller percentage provided in the company charter has the right to:

- Nominate candidates to the BOD and Supervisory Board.
- Examine and extract the book of minutes and resolutions of the BOD, mid-year and annual financial statements made according to VAS and reports of the Supervisory Board.
- Request convening of an extraordinary GMS in specified cases.
- Request the Supervisory Board to inspect each particular issue related to the company's management and administration.

3.3.2 Organizational Structure

JSCs may choose between two models:

1. GMS, BOD, Supervisory Board and GD. A Supervisory Board is not compulsory if the JSC has fewer than 11 shareholders and institutional shareholders own less than 50 percent of the JSC.

2. GMS, BOD and GD. In this case at least 20 percent of the members of the BOD must be independent members and the BOD must establish an "Independent Auditing Committee".

3.3.3 Corporate Governance

The General Meeting of Shareholders (GMS): The GMS is the JSC's highest decision-making body. In addition to the annual GMS within four months from the end of the financial year, the GMS may meet on an extraordinary basis. The annual GMS must at least debate and pass resolutions regarding:

- The annual financial statements and business plan of the JSC.
- The report of the BOD on the governance and results of operations and performance of each member of the BOD.
- The Report of the Supervisory Board on the business results of the company, results of performance of the BOD and GD.
- The self-evaluation reports on the operation of the Supervisory Board and performance of each Supervisory Board member.
- The dividend amounts payable on each type of share.

GMS quorum: The GMS and other shareholders' meetings need at least 51% of voting shares to be present to reach a quorum. If there is no quorum, within 30 days of the first meeting a second meeting is held. The second meeting requires 33% of voting shares to be present to reach a quorum. If still no quorum is reached, a third meeting will be held within 20 days without a required quorum.

GMS decisions: GMS resolutions shall be adopted if approved by a number of shareholders representing at least 51 percent of the total votes of all attending shareholders, except for resolutions on the following topics that require at least 65 percent: i) Types of shares and total number of shares of each type, ii) Change in business sectors, trades and fields, iii) Change in organizational and management structure of the company, iv) Investment projects or sale of assets equal to or more than 35 percent of the total value of company assets as per the latest financial statements of the company, or a smaller percentage or value provided by the company charter and v) Reorganization or dissolution of the company.

The Board of Directors (BOD): The BOD is the JSC's management body. Its term must not exceed five years and BOD members may be re-elected for an unlimited number of terms. The BOD has the following rights and obligations:

- To decide on the company's development strategies, annual business plans, investment plans and investment projects within the competence and limits prescribed by law.
- To decide on the organizational structure and internal management regulations of the company.
- To decide on the establishment of subsidiaries, branches and representative offices and the capital contribution to or purchase of shares from other enterprises.
- To recommend the types of shares and total number of shares of each type which may be offered, to decide on offering new

shares or raising funds in other forms, to decide on the selling prices of shares and bonds of the company and to decide on the redemption of shares.

- To decide on market expansion, marketing and technology.
- To approve contracts for purchase, sale, borrowing and lending and other contracts valued at 35 or more percent of the JSC's total value of assets.
- To appoint, remove or dismiss the chairperson of the BOD and to appoint, remove and sign / terminate contracts with the GD and other key managers of the company and to decide on salaries and other benefits of such managers.
- To appoint an authorized representative to participate in the MC or the GMS in another company and decide on the level of his/her remuneration and other benefits.
- To supervise and direct the GD and other managers.
- To approve the agenda and contents of documents for the GMS; to convene the GMS or to solicit written opinions for the General Meeting of Shareholders to pass decisions.
- To submit annual final financial statements to the GMS and to recommend dividends to be paid and the time limit and procedures for payment of dividends or for dealing with losses.
- To recommend reorganization or dissolution of the company or to request insolvency of the company.

The Chairperson of the Board of Directors: The BOD must elect a member of the BOD as its Chairperson. The Chairperson of the BOD may concurrently be the GD of the company. The Chairperson of the BOD has the following rights and obligations: i) To prepare working plans and programs of the BOD, ii) To prepare agendas, contents and documents for meetings of the BOD, iii) To convene and chair meetings of the BOD, iv) To organize the adoption of resolutions of the BOD, v) To monitor the implementation of resolutions of the Board of Directors and vi) To chair the GMS and meetings of the BOD.

The General Director: The BOD appoints or hires for a up to five years a GD, who manages day-to-day business of the company. The GD may be re-appointed for an unlimited number of terms. The GD is responsible for the day-to-day business operations of the company and decide on all matters that are not in the competence of the BOD or GMS. The GD's rights and obligations include: i) the implementation of decisions and resolutions of the BOD, ii) the organization and implementation of business plans and investment plans of the company, iii) proposing internal management regulations of the company, iv) appointing and removing managers and staff of the company, and v) deciding on salaries, wages and other benefits for company employees.

Supervisory Board: The Supervisory Board has between 3-5 members. The term of office of Supervisors must not exceed 5 years. Supervisors shall elect one of them to be the head of the Supervisory Board on the majority principle. The Supervisory Board must have more than half of its members permanently residing in Vietnam. The head of the Supervisory Board must be a professional accountant or auditor and work on a full-time basis in the company. A Supervisor must not be a family member (child, parent, sibling or spouse) of any member of the BOD, the GD or other manager in the company, and must not hold any other managerial position in the company. The Supervisory Board's main task is to supervise the BOD and the GD in the management of the company. Its rights and obligations include:

- To inspect the reasonableness, legality, truthfulness and prudence in the management and administration of business operations, the consistency and appropriateness of accounting and statistical work and preparation of financial statements.
- To appraise the completeness, legality and truthfulness of the company's business reports and annual and biannual financial statements, and reports evaluating management work of the BOD and to submit appraisal reports at the annual GMS.
- To review, inspect and evaluate the effect and efficiency of internal controls, audit and risk management and systems.
- To review the company's accounting books / entries and other company documents; to examine other business activities of the company when necessary, pursuant to a resolution of the GMS or if requested by a (group of) shareholder(s).
- To propose to the BOD or the GMS measures to modify, supplement and improve the company's organizational structure, its management, supervision or administration.

- When detecting that a member of the BOD or the GD violates the law, to send a written notice to the BOD and request the violator to stop the violation and take remedial measures.
- To participate in and discuss at the GMS, BOD or other company meetings and to consult the BOD before submitting reports, conclusions and recommendations to the GMS.

3.4 Other Foreign Presences

3.4.1 Representative Offices

Representative Offices (ROs) are the simplest form of presence for foreign investors in Vietnam. However, unlike LLCs or JSCs, they are not independent legal entities under Vietnamese laws. The practical importance of ROs has steadily decreased over the years, mainly because ROs are now strictly limited to:

- Exercising the function of a liaison office,
- Promoting the formulation of co-operative projects of a foreign business entity in Vietnam,
- Conducting market research activities.

Note that ROs must not conduct any business- or revenue-generating activities. Specifically, they are prohibited to enter into commercial contracts in their own name or even monitor the implementation of contracts concluded by their foreign headquarters (this requirement, however, has been violated in the past by many foreign entrepreneurs who have used ROs to monitor contract implementation in Vietnam). ROs must also not sublet their office, represent other business entities in Vietnam or do anything which is not specifically permitted under the RO legislation.

Therefore, rather than opening a RO, foreign companies will usually avoid opening a RO in Vietnam and operate from outside Vietnam for a while, without any legal presence, and then directly set up a FIE after they have decided that Vietnam is a suitable and profitable market for them.

3.4.2 Branches

Branches are not independent legal entities under Vietnamese laws. For ***foreign enterprises*** to open a branch in Vietnam it must have operated for at least five years since its legal establishment or valid business registration in the country of origin. In the past, foreign branches have been established primarily where foreign companies were not entitled to establishing an FIE in Vietnam (e.g., in the banking and airline sectors, which now is no longer the case). The practical relevance of foreign branches is therefore low in practice.

For ***domestic enterprises***, including FIEs, however, establishing of branches may be more useful. For example, where the FIE would like to operate all over Vietnam, it may set-up branches in different locations in Vietnam and operate them as separate accounting units without having to set-up additional legal entities with their numerous regulatory and administrative requirements.

3.4.3 Establishment

Art. 45 LOI provides that when establishing a domestic branch or representative office, the enterprise shall apply for branch/representative office registration to the business registration authority in charge. Such an application shall consist of:

- Notice of establishment of the branch/representative office;
- Copies of the establishment decision and minutes of the meeting on the establishment of the enterprise's branch/representative office, legal documents of the head of the branch/representative office.
- Within 03 working days from the receipt of the application, the business registration authority shall consider the validity of the application and decide whether to issue a "Certificate of Branch" / "Certificate of Representative Office Rgistration". The business registration authority will inform the applicant of necessary supplementation if the application is incomplete or provide a written explanation if the application is rejected.
- The enterprise shall apply for revision of the Certificate of Branch or Representative Office Registration within 10 days from which a change occurs.

Within 10 days from the decision on the business location, the enterprise shall send a notice of business location establishment to the business registration authority.

3.5 Business Cooperation Contracts

According to Art. 27 of the LOI, a Business Cooperation Contract (BCC) is an agreement between one or more foreign investors and one or more Vietnamese partners with the objective of cooperating to operate one or more specific business activities. The BCC does not require the parties to establish a new FIE, however during the execution of a BCC, the parties may reach an agreement on using assets derived from the business cooperation to establish an enterprise in accordance with the regulations of the LOE. The parties to a BCC shall establish a coordinating board to execute the BBC. Functions, tasks and powers of the coordinating board shall be agreed upon by the parties. A BCC must at least contain:

- Names, addresses and authorized representatives of parties to the BCC as well as business or project address,
- Objectives and scope of the BCC,
- Parties' contribution to the BCC, and distribution of business investment results between the parties,
- Rights and obligations of the BCC's parties,
- Schedule and duration of the BCC,
- Provisions on BCC adjustment, transfer and termination.
- Responsibilities for BCC breaches and dispute settlement.

The procedures for issuance of IRCs apply to BCCs signed between a domestic investor and a Foreign Investor, or between Foreign Investors. A foreign investor to a BCC may establish an operating office in Vietnam to execute the BCC. The location of the operating office shall be decided by the foreign investor depending on the requirements for BCC execution. The operating office has its own seal. The foreign investor may open a bank account, hire employees, sign contracts and carry out business activities under the BCC and its "Certificate of Registration."

3.6 Public Private Partnerships

3.6.1 Scope and Capital Requirements

Public-Private Partnership (PPP) investments are governed by the Law No. 64/2020/QH14 on Public-Private Partnership Investment ("PPP Law"). The PPP Law provides the rights, obligations and responsibilities of entities, organizations and individuals involved in PPP investments. Under Art. 4 (1) PPP Law, PPP investments are permitted in the following five sectors:

1. Transportation;
2. Power grids, power plants, except hydropower plants;
3. Water resources and irrigation, clean water supply, water drainage and wastewater treatment, waste management and waste disposal.
4. Healthcare, education and training.
5. Information Technology infrastructure.

Art. 4 (2) PPP Law requires the following minimum investment capital:

- A minimum capital requirement of not less than VND 200 billion applies to PPP projects in the above sectors, except for healthcare, education and training projects. If PPP projects are executed in areas facing socio-economic difficulties or extreme socio-economic difficulties as defined in the LOI, a minimum capital requirement of at least VND 100 billion applies instead.
- A minimum capital requirement of at least VND 100 billion applies to PPP projects in the healthcare, education and training sectors.

3.6.2 Types and Content

Art. 45 PPP Law provides for six types of standard PPP contracts:

Build - Operate - Transfer contract (BOT contract): Contract under which a PPP project investor or enterprise is assigned the right to build and operate infrastructure works and systems within a predetermined term; upon expiry of such term, the PPP project investor or enterprise transfers these works or systems to the State.

Build - Transfer - Operate contract (BTO contract): Contract under which a PPP project investor or enterprise is assigned the right to build infrastructure works and systems; after the construction is complete, the PPP project investor or enterprise transfers these works or systems to the State and is accorded the right to operate these works or systems within a specified period of time.

Build - Own - Operate contract (BOO contract): Contract under which a PPP project investor or enterprise is assigned the right to build, own and operate infrastructure works and systems within a predetermined term; upon expiry of such term, the PPP project investor or enterprise terminates the contract.

Operate - Manage contract (O&M contract): O&M contract means a contract under which a PPP project investor or enterprise is assigned the right to operate and manage part or the whole of existing infrastructure works and systems within a predetermined term; upon expiry of such term, the PPP project investor or enterprise terminates the contract.

Build - Transfer - Lease contract (BTL contract): BTL contract means the contract under which a PPP project investor or enterprise is assigned the right to build infrastructure works or systems and transfer them after completion; is accorded the right to supply public products and services on the basis of operating and exploiting these works or systems within a predetermined term; the transferee signs a service lease and pays the PPP project investor or enterprise.

Build - Lease - Transfer contract (BLT contract): BLT contract means the contract under which a PPP project investor or enterprise is assigned the right to build infrastructure works or systems and supply public products and services on the basis of operating and exploiting these works or systems within a specified period of time; the transferee-to-be signs a service lease and pays the PPP project investor or enterprise; upon expiry of such term, the PPP project investor or enterprise transfers these works or systems to the State.

Mixed contracts are possible and contain elements of different standard contracts as mentioned above.

The Government provides sample contracts (templates) applicable to each of the above contract types, which are the basis on which the parties will negotiate the specific legal, financial and other commercial terms of the contemplated PPP investment. Deviations from the Government templates is possible in theory; however, Art. 47 PPP Law requires that any PPP contract must contain at least the following information and terms:

- Objectives, scale, location and schedule of implementation of a project; time and duration of an infrastructure work or system; the effective date of the contract; contract term;
- Scope of and requirements concerning engineering, technology and quality of the infrastructure work or system, supplied public products or services;
- Total investment; capital structure; financial plan, including the financial arrangement plan; public product and service prices and charges, including methods and formulas for setting or adjusting them; state capital invested in a PPP project and the corresponding form of management and use (if any);
- Conditions for use of land and other natural resources; plans to organize the construction of auxiliary works; requirements for compensation, support and resettlement; assurance of safety and environmental protection; force majeure cases and plans for response to force majeure events;

- Responsibilities for carrying out licensing procedures according to regulations of relevant laws; design; organization of construction; quality inspection, supervision and management at the construction phase; acceptance testing, settlement of investment capital and confirmation of the completion of infrastructure works and systems; provision of main input materials used for production and business activities of the project;
- Responsibilities for the operation and commercial use of infrastructure works and systems so that public products and services are provided in a continuous and stable manner; conditions, order and procedures for transfer of infrastructure works and systems;
- Performance security; rights of ownership, management, and exploitation of assets related to the project; rights and obligations of the PPP project investor or enterprise; the agreement on use of a third-party guarantee service with respect to the obligations of the contract signatory;
- Plans for contract performance in response to the substantially changing circumstances; response, compensation and punitive measures in case of contract breaches;
- Responsibilities of parties related to information security; reporting regime; provision of information and related documents and explanations about the contract performance at the request of competent authorities;

- Principles and conditions for contract amendment, supplementation and termination prior to expiry; assignment of parties' rights and obligations; the lender's rights; procedures, rights and obligations of the parties upon contract discharge;
- Investment incentives, guarantees, revenue increase and decrease, assurance of balancing of foreign currencies, types of insurance (if any);
- Governing law and dispute resolution mechanism.

3.6.3 PPP Guarantees

According to Art. 77 (1) PPP Law, the investor's equity contribution must be at least 15% of total investment in a PPP-project. In addition, Art. 48 (1)-(3) PPP Law PPP require that the PPP project investor must provide a contract performance security before the effective date of the contract.

Prior to contract conclusion, Art. 33 (1) PPP Law requires a bid guarantee amounting to 0.5-1.5% of total investment in the project. Bid solicitors must return or release bid guarantees to unsuccessfully bidding investors within the time limit specified in the invitation for bid, but not longer than 14 days from the date on which the results of investor selection are approved. With regard to the selected investor, their bid guarantee shall be returned or released after the PPP project enterprise established by the investor has fulfilled their obligations specified in the contract performance security (or performance bond) as prescribed in Art. 48 PPP Law. Bid guarantees shall not be returned if: i) investors withdraw their bids during the validity of these bids; ii) the investor violates the law on bidding to the extent that such violation leads to the bid cancellation, iii) the investor has not conducted or refused to negotiate or finalize the contract within 30 days of receipt of the bid-winning notice from the bid solicitor, or has negotiated and finalized the contract but refused to sign the contract, except in force majeure cases or iv) PPP project enterprises established by investors have failed to fulfil their obligations specified in the contract performance security (or performance bond).

Based on the scale and nature of each project, the value of a contract performance security shall be specified in the invitation for bid at a determined rate of between 1-3% of total investment in the project. The validity period of the contract performance security shall start on the effective date of the contract and end on the date on which the PPP project enterprise completes its contractual obligations during the stage of construction of infrastructure work or system under the contract; In cases where it is necessary to prolong the construction period.

The PPP project investor shall be entitled to return or release the contract performance security after discharge of their contractual obligation to build the construction work or infrastructure system.

3.6.4 Foreign currency balancing guarantee

For significant PPP projects, i.e., those under the investment policy decisions of the National Assembly and the Prime Minister, Art. 81 PPP Law stipulate that PPP investors who have exercised their right to buy foreign currency to meet the needs of current, capital and other transactions, or transfer capital, profits, or other liquidated investments remitted abroad and who cannot accommodate their legal foreign currency demands, shall be entitled to use up to 30% of VND revenues generated from each project after deduction of VND spending amounts as a guarantee for foreign currency balancing.

3.6.5 Sharing of PPP Project Revenues

Art. 82 (1) PPP Law provides that if the actual project revenue is 125% higher than the revenue specified in the financial plan under a PPP project contract, the investor and the PPP project enterprise will share with the State 50% of the difference between the actual revenue and 125% of revenue in the financial plan. The increased revenue may be shared after adjustment in the prices and costs of public products and services or the PPP contract term according to the provisions of Art. 50, 51 and 65 of the PPP Law and must be audited by the State Audit.

If the actual project revenue is 75% lower than the revenue specified in the financial plan under a PPP project contract, the State will share with the investor or PPP project enterprise 50% of the difference between 75% of revenue in the financial plan and the actual revenue. Sharing of reduced revenues may occur if the following requirements are satisfied:

- Projects are developed and executed under BOT, BTO or BOO contracts;
- Changes in relevant planning, policies and laws result in a reduction in revenue;

- Measures to adjust prices and charges of public products and services, and PPP contract terms, according to the provisions of Articles 50, 51 and 65 of this Law, have been fully taken, but the minimum revenue requirement of 75% has not been met yet;
- The reduced revenue has been audited by the State Audit.

3.6.6 Dispute Resolution

According to Art. 97 PPP Law, disputes between investors with at least one foreign investor; disputes between investors or PPP project enterprises and foreign organizations or individuals shall be settled by: i) Vietnamese Arbitration; ii) Vietnamese Court; iii) Overseas Arbitration; iv) International Arbitration or v) Arbitration established under agreements between disputing parties' agreement. As far as a Vietnamese state authority is party to a dispute, only Vietnamese Arbitration or Vietnamese Courts are available. Negotiation and sometimes mediation may be agreed between the parties which precede arbitration or court proceedings.

However, Art. 55 PPP Law requires that a PPP project contract *"signed between a Vietnamese state authority and a PPP project investor or enterprise shall be governed under Vietnamese legislation."* This is problematic as many foreign project investors are reluctant to agree to Vietnamese laws because they will be more familiar with common law jurisdictions such as English or Singaporean law, which govern many international PPP projects.

3.7 Mergers & Acquisitions

3.7.1 Licensing Requirements

Mergers & Acquisitions (M&A) in Vietnam are governed by the LOI, the LOE and by the general principles of the Vietnamese Civil Code. Certain M&A transactions may in addition be subject to merger control under the Competition Law No. 23/2018/QH14 (LOC) and its implementing Decree No. 35/2020/ND-CP (Decree 35). The LOI/LOE acknowledge foreign investors' rights to invest in Vietnamese companies. The acquisition of capital contributions or shares in a Vietnamese company operating in certain conditional sectors, for instance in the banking, financial services and insurance industries, is further regulated by specialized laws complementing the provisions of the LOI/LOE. Foreign investors must only obtain an IRC according to the licensing procedures in the LOI if their acquisition of (or subscription to) LLC capital contributions or JSC shares:

- Increases the permitted foreign ownership ratio in Vietnamese companies conducting business in certain conditional or restricted business sectors.
- Results in the foreign investor, after closing of the transaction, holding 50% or more of the LLC's or JSC's Charter Capital, except in cases in which a 100% Vietnamese enterprise is acquired. In such case, only the ERC must be obtained. However

the foreign investor must in such cases apply for a an "Investment Policy Approval" (IPA) prior to executing the transaction (see 2.4 above).

- Results in co-owning economic organizations which LURs in island and border or coastal communes, wards and towns or in other areas affecting national defense and security.

The above applies regardless of whether the acquisition of capital contributions in the Vietnamese LLC or the shares in a Vietnamese JSC follows a purchase from an existing investor or by way of capital increase. Based on the above, it is not required to conduct additional investment procedures under the LOI upon transferring contributed capital or shares between foreign investors if the ownership percentage of foreign investors remains unchanged.

3.7.2 Share- and Asset Deal

Acquisition of shares / capital contributions ("share deal"):

The share deal is the most common M&A transaction, in which the purchaser acquires from the seller capital contributions in a LLC or shares in a JSC, either by way of acquiring existing capital contribution / shares or by way of subscription to newly issued capital contributions or shares in case of capital increases and (public) offering of shares. Sometimes, the purchaser will also acquire newly-issued shares of a public company by way of subscription or otherwise shares or share options from existing shareholders of a company. The share deal has the advantage that the purchaser acquires from the seller automatically not only all assets but also all licenses and contracts that the target company has obtained or concluded. The share deal also allows Foreign Investors the acquisition of certain types of assets that cannot be sold to them as individual assets in an asset deal, such as e.g., land (LURs), certain real estate and related fixtures). However, a share deal also means that the purchaser automatically acquires the target's liabilities, which means that the purchaser needs to conduct a thorough due diligence before signing a Share Purchase Agreement ("SPA") / Share Subscription Agreement ("SSA") in cases of capital increases.

Acquisition of assets (asset deal):

Investors may also acquire a Vietnamese target company by way of purchasing the entirety of the target's assets, but not the target's liabilities. For above state reasons, this type of M&A transaction is less common in Vietnam than a share deal. There are no licensing requirements with regards to amending the IRC in an asset deal, as the ownership structure remains unchanged. While the purchaser does not automatically acquire the target company's liabilities, the asset deal is more complicated with regards to transferring the target's contracts, as every single contract needs the consent of the other contract party. In addition, operational licenses and permits are not automatically transferred to the purchaser and must be newly applied for. One of the advantages of an asset deal is that accounting-wise, the purchaser is able to depreciate the purchase price of the assets over the remaining accounting life of the acquired target assets.

3.7.3 M&A Transaction Procedures

Memorandum of Understanding ("MOU"):

Once the investor has identified an acquisition target, and the company owner is willing to sell, purchaser and seller acquirer will usually sign a "Memorandum of Understanding" ("MOU") in which the parties express their willingness to enter into the transaction and lay out the basic terms and timelines of the prospective transaction. While the MOU is only binding if it expressly states so (unusual), it is an important "symbolic" document that provides clarity and documents the commitment and seriousness of the parties to the MOU. Usual contents of the MOU that seller and purchaser will address, include: i) a description of the target and ownership, ii) existing encumbrances, iii) scope and time of the due diligence, iv) purchase price components and determination, v) timelines for signing, executing and closing of the transaction, vi) exclusivity, vii) termination. In most transactions, confidential information will be disclosed by both parties therefore it is common practice that the MOU also includes a confidentiality provision with regards to both the transaction and the information revealed in the due diligence.

Due diligence of target company:

A thorough due diligence of the target company is essential for the purchaser to identify any hidden liabilities or other legal-, tax or commercial/financial issues with the target company. For private companies, the purchaser's main source of information will be documents and information provided by the target company's owners. The scope and depth of the due diligence usually depends on the business of the company and the size of the transaction. Generally, a purchaser in a share deal conducts at least a legal due diligence covering ownership structure, third-party rights, existence and validity of licenses, assessment of contract risks as well as existing and potential liabilities and litigation.

In addition, a financial due diligence is essential in which the accounts and financial data of the target company need to be verified. However, in practice it is often hard to obtain complete and accurate information, as bookkeeping and transparency standards in Vietnamese domestic companies are often below international standards. This is particularly true with regards to accounting information, as keeping different sets of financial data for different recipients is still not uncommon.

Share Purchase Agreement / Sale and Purchase Agreement:

After successful due diligence, seller and purchaser will negotiate, in a share deal, the Share Purchase Agreement and in an asset deal, the Sale and Purchase Agreement relating to the target's assets (both: "SPA"). In both cases, the SPA is the formal agreement that sets out the terms and conditions relating to the sale and purchase of shares in or assets of the target company. If the acquisition relates to less than 100% of the target company's capital contributions/shares and therefore old shareholders remain, a Shareholders' Agreement ("SA") will often complement the SPA. The SA regulates the rights and obligations of old and new shareholders amongst each other after closing of the transaction. The new shareholders will often request tag-along and drag-along clauses in the target company's company charter, allowing them to force the old shareholders, under certain conditions, to sell their remaining shares to themselves or third parties. While these clauses are international standard, Vietnamese shareholders are often unfamiliar with them.

The SPA should very clearly set out what is being sold, to whom and for how much, other obligations and liabilities as well as representations and warranties. The latter are particularly important where the due diligence was limited in scope and/or based on incomplete documentation. The purchase price provisions should address not only the composition and calculation of the purchase price, but also how the price will be satisfied, when the price must be paid and whether the price is a fixed sum, or subject to a price adjustment mechanism. A tax covenant / indemnity offers the purchaser protection for any tax liabilities that may not have been revealed by the due diligence. In certain situations, it may be necessary for the completion of the SPA to be conditional on certain matters, such as obtaining tax clearances or regulatory approval. In such cases, a "conditions precedent" or "closing conditions" clause will usually be added into the SPA. This is also true if the purchase price or closing of the transaction depends on certain outcomes of the due diligence that will only be available later. In this context, the SPA will often include a "material adverse change" clause which is generally known and not uncommon in Vietnam. Overall, the completion / closing mechanics can be difficult as the parties will need to agree upon timings, place of completion, the actions and what is to be delivered at completion. The latter normally include the post-completion formalities such as amending the company's IRC/ERC.

3.8 Common Formation Mistakes

- ***Using a Vietnamese nominee to establish a company:*** In order to avoid the delays and complications in getting a company established (specifically to circumvent the IRC procedures), a Vietnamese individual is asked to establish the company as the sole owner (on behalf of the foreigner/foreign entity), with the intention that the ownership of the Vietnamese company will subsequently be transferred to the foreigner/foreign entity. This is problematic, because "nominee-agreements" are invalid and thus unenforceable in Vietnam.
- ***Missing the 90-day timeline to pay the Charter Capital:*** The Charter Capital of the FIE must be transferred to the FIE's DIA within 90 days after the ERC has been issued. The foreign currency amount transferred must match exactly the agreed Charter Capital in VND as mentioned in the company's ERC. Failure to transfer within 90 days can have significant consequences for the company, including revocation of the ERC.
- ***Private loans to the FIE:*** If loans to the FIE are proceeded through private bank accounts rather than the DIA, the loan will not be able to be deposited back into the Foreign Investor's personal bank account. The Foreign Investor is then stuck with VND cash if the FIE repays. Therefore, investors should always loan funds to the FIE from abroad from their bank account into the FIE's DIA.

- ***Residency requirement for one legal representative:*** Each company in Vietnam requires at least one LR, and at least one LR must reside in Vietnam. This means: If one LR is permanently residing outside of Vietnam, a second LR needs to be appointed.

- ***Not registering promptly for tax:*** Tax registration is important, and it is time sensitive to avoid penalties. Also, if you don't undertake your tax registration and VAT election promptly, you may not be able to enter the VAT credit system for the first year, denying you the ability to receive refunds or VAT credits to carry forward.

- ***Undocumented or unregistered loans:*** Loans from abroad must go through the DIA which will ensure loans can be repaid back to where they came. Loans from domestic sources can be made into the company's current bank account. However, loans that are not documented with proper loan agreements are often regarded as revenue by the tax authorities and taxed accordingly. Foreign currency loans with a term of at least 12 months loans that are not registered with the State Bank of Vietnam can potentially result in the loss of the ability to repatriate the loans and the loans becoming taxable revenue to the company.

- ***Not appointing a chief accountant:*** Even though not mandatory for companies with less than 10 employees, appointing a n experienced Chief Accountant can be instrumental in securing financial compliance.

4. Taxation

4.1 Overview

Foreign investors and entrepreneurs doing business in Vietnam are subject to corporate income tax (CIT), foreign contractor tax (FCT), value added tax (VAT), personal income tax (PIT) and in some cases, the special sales tax (SST) as well as certain import duties (in case of trade). Vietnam has also developed a legal framework for transfer pricing. In some cases, double taxation may occur. Double Tax Avoidance Agreements (DTAs) eliminate double taxation in specific cases by identifying exemptions or reducing the amount of taxes payable in Vietnam for residents of the signatories of the agreements. Vietnam has signed DTAs with more than 80 countries. It is crucial for foreign investors, entrepreneurs doing business or expatriates working in Vietnam to be aware of such applicable DTAs in their case, and to understand the requirements to apply these DTAs in practice with the Vietnamese tax authorities (which is not always easy).

4.2 Corporate Income Tax

4.2.1 Calculation

CIT applies to the foreign investor's taxable income, defined as total revenue within one tax period plus other relevant income (including income received from outside of Vietnam) minus deductible expenses and losses carried forward. CIT payable then equals the taxable income multiplied by the applicable CIT rate. The standard CIT rate is 20%, except for companies operating in the oil- and gas as well as the mining sector which are subject to CIT rates ranging from 32% to 50%.

Taxpayers may carry forward their full tax losses consecutively for up to five years. Losses arising from incentivised activities can be offset against profits from non-incentivised activities, and vice versa. However, a carry back of losses is not permitted. Vietnam does not recognize consolidating losses against profits on a group level but allows offsetting only within the specific legal entity even if they are 100% subsidiaries or related companies.

Deductible expenses include all expenses required for revenue generation, which are evidenced by proper documentation (including e.g., bank transfer vouchers where the invoice value is VND 20 million or above) and not specifically identified as being non-deductible, including::

- Depreciation of fixed assets in violation of applicable laws.
- R&D reserves in violation of applicable laws.
- Contributions to voluntary pension funds and life insurance for employees exceeding VND 3 million per month per person.
- Employee remuneration which is not paid or not stated in the employment contract or collective labour agreement.
- Severance payments exceeding the labour law provisions.
- Staff welfare exceeding a cap of one month's average salary, including non- compulsory medical and accident insurance.

- Overhead expenses allocated to a permanent establishment in Vietnam by the foreign company's head office which exceed the permitted amount under a prescribed revenue-based allocation formula.
- Loan interest proportionally to any charter capital not yet contributed.
- Loan interest from non-economic and non-credit organisations exceeding 1.5 times the interest rate set by the SBV.
- Interest payments exceeding 30% of EBITDA.
- Provisions for stock devaluation, bad debts, financial investment losses, product warranties or construction work in violation of applicable regulations.
- Unrealised foreign exchange losses due to the year-end revaluation of foreign currency items other than accounts payable.
- Donations except for certain donations for education, health care, natural disaster or building charitable homes for the poor or for scientific research.
- Administrative penalties, fines, late payment interest.
- Service fees paid to related parties that do not meet certain conditions.

For insurance companies, securities trading and lotteries, the Ministry of Finance provides specific guidance on deductible expenses.

4.2.2 Administration

The default tax year is the calendar year. Companies are required to make quarterly provisional CIT payments based on estimates. The provisional CIT payments in the first three quarters of a tax year must not account for less than 75% of the final CIT liability for the year. Any shortfall is subject to late payment interest of up to 11% p.a., counting from the payment deadline for quarter three provisional CIT. Companies must submit their final CIT returns and pay the outstanding CIT amount annually not later than the last day of the third month after the fiscal year end.

4.2.3 Capital Gains Tax

Profits resulting from the sale of capital contributions or shares in a Vietnamese company are generally subject to 20% CIT. Although no separate tax type, this is often referred to as "capital assignment (profit) tax" or "capital gains tax". The taxable gain is the ***sales proceeds and purchase cost (or the initial nominal value of the charter capital or shares contributed) minus applicable transfer expenses.*** Where the seller is a foreign entity, a Vietnamese purchaser is required to withhold the capital gains tax from the payment to the seller on behalf of the Vietnamese tax authorities. Where the purchaser is also a foreign entity, the Vietnamese entity which is transferred can ultimately be held responsible for the tax payment.

Tax declaration and payment is required within 10 calendar days from the date the parties sign the SPA, or, if official approvals are required, within 10 calendar days from such approval. Vietnamese tax authorities may adjust the purchase price for capital gains tax purposes where they believe that the purchase price is not at arm's length or where the purchase price is deemed too low and "hiding" another transaction. Whether not only the transfer of a Vietnamese entity, but also the transfer of an overseas parent (direct or indirect) of a Vietnamese company is subject to capital gains tax is disputed, with Vietnamese tax authorities often taking a broad approach to taxation. Capital gains of a local entity from the transfer of securities are taxed at 20%, except for capital gains resulting from the transfer of public companies or publicly listed securities by a foreign entity are taxed at 0.1% of the total sales proceeds.

4.2.4 Transfer Pricing Rules

Related party transactions may be subject to Vietnamese transfer pricing (TP) rules which are governed by Decree 132/2020/ND-CP (Decree 132). Vietnamese tax authorities have over the last years significantly increased the enforcement of TP regulations, taking pro-active steps to monitor related party transactions and inspect enterprises to secure compliance.

Related party definition and threshold: Related party transactions covered by Decree 132 include: "*purchase, sale, bartering, renting, leasing out, borrowing, lending, transfer or disposal of commodities, provision of services; financial borrowing, lending, financial services, financial guarantee and other financial instruments; purchase, sale, bartering, renting, leasing out, borrowing, lending, transfer or disposition of tangible assets, intangible assets and agreement on purchase, sale and sharing of resources such as assets, capital, labour and sharing of costs between related parties.*"

Parties are related if, amongst others, i) a party is directly or indirectly involved in the management, control of, contribution of capital to, or investment in, the other party or ii) parties are directly or indirectly affected by the management, control of, contribution of capital, or investment, from the other party. The following thresholds and control requirements apply:

- An enterprise participates directly or indirectly in at least 25% of the other enterprise's equity;
- Each of the two enterprises has at least 25% of its equity held, whether directly or indirectly, by a third party;
- An enterprise is the shareholder having the greatest ownership interest in the other enterprise, or participates (in)directly in at least 10% of total share capital of the other enterprise;
- An enterprise guarantees or offers another enterprise a loan under any form to the extent that the loan amount equals at least 25% of equity of the borrowing enterprise and makes up for more than 50% of total medium- and long-term debts of the borrowing enterprise.

TP methods and determination of comparables: These include cost-plus, resale-price, profit-split and comparable profits methods. Intercompany agreements using cost-plus should define as precisely as possible the services and pricing to avoid confusion with regards to the service provider's independent position. In this regard, Decree 132 sets the acceptable arm's length range from the 35th to the 75th percentile, with the median value at the 50th percentile.

When determining comparable prices, taxpayers must determine comparables in the following order: (i) the taxpayer's internal comparables, (ii) comparables in the same country/market, and (iii) comparables in regional countries with similar industrial and economic standards and stage of development. Decree 132 gives the tax authorities the power to use their internal databases for TP assessment in case they find the comparables used by the taxpayer insufficient or in violation of Decree 132. Complementing this, Decree 132 also requires that TP analysis follows the "substance-over-form" rule according to which the tax authorities must determine tax liability by analysing the substance of a related party transaction rather than simply looking at its form. The tax authorities have become increasingly more sophisticated with challenging comparables used by taxpayers and are also performing increasing numbers of TP audits in case they suspect that the taxpayer had submitted incomplete or inaccurate TP documentation.

Deductible loan interest: Under Decree 132, the total loan interest cost arising after deducting deposit interests and lending interests within a specific taxable period which is deducted during the process of determination of income subject to the corporate income tax is capped at 30% of the net profit generated from business activities within the taxable period plus loan interest costs arising after deducting deposit interests and lending interests arising within the taxable period plus depreciation/amortization expenses arising within that period of a taxpayer (EBITDA). The portion of loan interest cost which is non-deductible may be carried forward to the next taxable period for the determination of total loan interest cost deductible if total loan interest cost deductible in the next taxable period is lower than the amount prescribed in point a of this clause. The loan interest costs may be carried forward for a maximum consecutive period of five years. Excluded from the cap are i) loans of taxpayers that are credit institutions or insurance companies, ii) ODA loans and concessional loans of the Government which are granted to enterprises in the on-lending form; iii) loans intended for implementing certain national target and welfare programs.

TP documentation: As far as an intercompany agreement constitutes a related party transaction, certain documentation requirements must be met. These include an annual declaration of related party transactions and TP methodology used, and a taxpayer confirmation of the arm's length value of their transactions (or otherwise the making of voluntary adjustments). Decree 132 requires that the TP method applied does not result in a decrease of tax liabilities to the state budget. Taxpayers with related party transactions must prepare and maintain a comprehensive TP documentation, containing a master file, a local file and country-by-country report. Decree 132 contains a TP declaration form which requires disclosure of detailed information, including segmentation of profit and loss by related party and third-party transactions. The TP declaration forms must be submitted together with the annual CIT return. Under Decree 132, a taxpayer is exempt from preparing transfer pricing documentation if one of the following conditions is met:

- Revenue below VND 50 billion and total value of related party transactions below VND 30 billion in a tax period, or
- Conclusion of an Advance Pricing Agreement (APA) and submission of annual APA report(s), or

- Revenue below VND 200 billion and achieving at least the following ratios of earnings before interest and tax to revenue from the following businesses: distribution (5%), manufacturing (10%), processing (15%), or
- Taxpayers with only domestic related party transactions, with their related parties having the same tax rate and none of the parties enjoy tax incentives.

4.3 Foreign Contractor Tax

4.3.1 Scope

FCT applies to foreign companies and individuals without a legal presence in Vietnam which earn income sourced from Vietnam on the basis of agreements with Vietnamese parties (including FIEs). In such cases, FCT is levied on payments received by the foreign contractor from Vietnam. The FCT is not a separate tax, but a combination of VAT and CIT, or PIT for income of foreign individuals.

Exempt from FCT is the pure supply of goods (i.e. where risk and responsibility for goods passes prior to such goods entering Vietnam and there are no goods-related services performed in Vietnam), services performed and consumed outside Vietnam and various other services performed wholly outside Vietnam (e.g. certain repairs, training, advertising, promotion, etc.).

Who bears the FCT in practice: *While the Vietnamese contract partner is legally obliged to withhold the FCT on the foreign party's behalf, the contract parties can stipulate in their contract that the FCT shall eventually be fully or partly borne by the Vietnamese side, for example as follows: "The Parties agree that Party A shall not only fully withhold the FCT on Consultant's behalf but also cover 50% of the applicable FCT on top of service fees agreed between the Parties, Party B shall cover only the remaining 50% of the applicable FCT."*

4.3.2 Rates

The following FCT rates apply:

Service or Income	Deemed VAT	Deemed CIT or PIT	
Supply and distribution of goods in Vietnam where seller's responsibility exceeds the pure supply of goods to border and passing of full risk to buyer at border gate	Exempt	1%	0.5%
Services not exclusively performed and consumed outside of Vietnam	5%	5%	1.5% or 2%
Services together **with** supply of machines or equipment	3%	2%	2%
Construction, installation **without** supply of materials, machinery or equipment	5%	2%	2%
Leasing of machinery and/or equipment	5%	5%	5%
Lease of aircraft, aircraft engines, aircraft spare parts and sea vessels	5%	2%	5%
Restaurant, hotel and casino management services	5%	10%	N/A
Logistics and transportation services	3%	2%	
Interest on loans	Exempt	5%	5%
Royalty income	Exempt	10%	5%
Transfer of securities, deposit certificates, and reinsurance commissions	Exempt	0.1%	
Insurance services	Exempt	5%	5%
Financial derivatives services	Exempt	2%	2%
Other services	2%	2%	1%

A withholding tax of 5% CIT applies to interest paid on loans from foreign entities. Offshore loans provided by certain government or semi-government institutions may be exempted from FCT under applicable double taxation or inter-governmental agreements. Interest paid on bonds (except for tax exempt bonds) and certificates of deposit issued to foreign entities is subject to 5% withholding tax. A 10% royalty withholding tax applies in the case of payments made to a foreign party for transfers of industrial property rights. However, if the transfer of patents, technical know-how or technology processes is used as part of the capital contribution of a Foreign Investor, no FCWT applies.

With regards to transactions in which Vietnamese individuals purchase goods or services from overseas suppliers conducting e-commerce and digital-based business activities, banks and payment intermediary service companies are required i) to withhold and pay tax on behalf of the e-commerce foreign contractors on a monthly basis (if such contractors do not register to pay tax in Vietnam and ii) to keep records of overseas remittances and provide this information monthly to the tax authorities if the Vietnamese individual customers use a payment forms for which withholding is not possible, specifically credit cards.

4.3.3 Double Taxation Agreements

FCT payable may be affected by double taxation agreements (DTAs), of which Vietnam has signed over 80 with a number of others at various stages of negotiation. While DTAs are in force with most EU countries, the signed DTA with the United States of America has not come into force yet.

Guidelines on the application of DTAs include regulations relating to beneficial ownership and anti-avoidance provisions. Under those guidelines, DTA benefits will be denied where the main purpose of an arrangement is to obtain beneficial treatment under the terms of a DTA or where the income receiver is not the beneficial owner. In this respect, the guidelines require a "substance over form analysis" for beneficial ownership.

Taxpayers who want to claim DTA relief must request the tax authority to approve DTA eligibility of their individual claim / case. The tax authority in charge must then review and assess DTA eligibility within 40 days upon receipt of the taxpayer's approval request. After that timeline, the tax department must issue a decision to either approve the amount of tax eligible for DTA exemption or reduction, or notify the taxpayer in writing about the reasons for rejection.

4.3.3 Payment Methods

Foreign contractors can, depending on their legal setup, choose among the following FCT payment methods:

- ***Deduction Method:*** Foreign contractors can apply for the deduction method if they (i) have a permanent establishment in Vietnam or are a tax resident in Vietnam, ii) the duration of the project in Vietnam is 182 days or more, and (iii) they adopt VAS accounting and obtain both tax registration and tax code. The Vietnamese customer is required to notify the tax office that the foreign contractor will pay tax under the deduction method within 20 working days from the date of signing the contract. If the foreign contractor carries out multiple projects in Vietnam and qualifies for application of the deduction method for one project, the contractor is required to apply the deduction method for its other projects as well. The foreign contractor will pay 20% CIT.

- *Direct Method:* For the direct method, due FCT will be withheld by the Vietnamese customer at various rates depending on the activities performed (see table above 4.2.2). The VAT part of the FCT withheld by the Vietnamese customer is generally an allowable input credit in its VAT return. Separate requirements for FCT declarations under this method are provided for foreign contractors providing goods and services for exploration, development and production of oil and gas.
- *Hybrid Method:* Allows foreign contractors to register / pay VAT based on the deduction method but pay CIT under the direct method. Foreign contractors wishing to apply the hybrid method must: i) Have a PE or be tax resident in Vietnam, ii) operate in Vietnam under a contract with a term of more than 182 days, and iii) maintain accounting records in accordance with the VAS.

4.4 Value Added Tax

4.4.1 Scope and Rates

VAT applies to goods and services used for production, trading and consumption in Vietnam. Vietnamese companies must charge VAT on the value of goods or services supplied in Vietnam. VAT also applies on the duty paid value of imported goods. The importer must pay VAT to customs authorities at the same time they pay import duties. For imported services, VAT is applied via the FCT mechanism.

VAT payable is calculated as the output VAT charged to customers less the input VAT on purchases of goods and services. The following VAT rates and exemptions apply:

VAT	Applied to
0%	Certain exported goods and services sold to overseas or non-tariff areas and consumed outside of Vietnam or in non-tariff areas, certain goods processed for export, goods sold to duty free shops, certain exported services, construction and installation carried out for export processing enterprises, aviation, marine and international transportation services. Application of the 0% rate requires complete and proper documentation, such as contracts, evidence of non-cash payment and customs documents. Not applied to some services such as, e.g., advertising-, training-, entertainment-, hotel- and tourism services provided in Vietnam to foreign customers and services relating to trade and distribution of goods.
5%	Provision of essential goods and services, including, amongst others, clean water, certain educational and teaching materials, books and certain publications, certain unprocessed food, medicine and medical equipment, certain rubber products, sugar, husbandry feed, various agricultural products and services, certain technical and scientific services as well as certain cultural-, artistic- and sport related products and services.
10%	All other goods, services and activities not specified as VAT non-subjected, VAT exempted or subject to VAT rates of 0% or 5%.

No output VAT is charged but input VAT may be credited, amongst others, in case of: i) compensation, bonuses and subsidies (except those provided in exchange for certain services), ii) transfer of emission rights and certain other financial revenues, iii) certain services rendered by foreign companies which do not have a permanent establishment in Vietnam and if the services are rendered outside of Vietnam (including repairs to means of transport, machinery or equipment, advertising, marketing, promotion of investment and trade), iv) overseas brokerage activities for the sale of goods and services overseas, v) transfer of investment projects, vi) capital contributions in kind, vii) commissions from the sale of exempt goods/services and vii) goods exported and then re-imported to Vietnam due to sales returns by overseas.

VAT exemptions include: i) some agricultural products, ii) goods/services provided by individuals having an annual revenue of VND 100 million or below, iii) transfer of land use rights, iv) financial derivatives and credit services (including credit card issuance, finance leasing and factoring), v) various securities activities including fund management, vi) capital assignment, foreign currency trading and debt factoring, vii) certain insurance services, viii) medical services, care services for the elderly and disabled, ix) printing and publishing of newspapers, magazines and certain types of books, x) passenger transport by public buses, xi) transfer of technology, software and software services except exported software which is entitled to 0% rate and xii) imports of machinery, equipment and materials which cannot be produced in Vietnam for direct use in scientific research and technology development activities.

Administration: All organizations and individuals producing or trading goods and services in Vietnam must register for VAT. In certain cases, branches of an enterprise must register separately and declare VAT on their own activities. Taxpayers must file VAT returns on a monthly basis by the 20th day of the subsequent month, or on a quarterly basis by the 30th day of the subsequent quarter (for companies with prior year annual revenue of VND 50 billion or less).

4.4.2 VAT Invoices

For input VAT to be creditable, taxpayers must always obtain a proper VAT invoice. Since 1st July 2022, electronic invoices (E-Invoices) are mandatory for full tax deductibility. All VAT invoices must contain certain mandatory items and be registered with or notified to the local tax authorities before they can be used. For exported goods, commercial invoices are used instead of domestic tax invoices. All companies using E-invoices without verification code must transfer their E-invoice data to the tax authorities, either directly or via an authorized E-invoicing service provider.

Certain “high tax risk companies” are required to use E-Invoices with a verification code for 12 months. High tax risk companies are defined as companies which have a charter capital of less than 15 billion VND and additional features, such as: i) sales of goods or provision of services to related parties, or ii) non-compliance with certain tax declaration requirements, or iii) change of their business location more than 2 times within 12 months without any notification or any tax declaration at the new location, or iv) companies subject to penalties for breach of invoice regulations in the last year. The "high tax risk company" status will be reassessed after 12 months for possible approval to use E-invoices without verification code.

4.4.3 VAT Refunds

VAT refunds are only granted in certain cases, including:

- Exporters having excess input VAT credits over 300 million VND. The refunds are provided on a monthly or quarterly basis, in line with the VAT declaration period of the taxpayer. The amount of input VAT relating to export sales (meeting the criteria for VAT refunds) that can be refunded to a taxpayer must not exceed 10% of its export revenue. VAT refunds are available to companies which import goods and then export them without further processing subject to various conditions.
- New projects of companies adopting VAT deduction method which are in the pre-operation investment phase and have accumulated VAT credits over VND 300 million VND. Exceptions include conditional investment projects which do not satisfy the regulated investment conditions, or investment projects of companies whose charter capital has not yet been contributed as regulated.
- Certain ODA projects, diplomatic exemption, foreigners buying goods in Vietnam for consumption overseas.

In other cases where a taxpayer's input VAT for a period exceeds its output VAT, it must carry the excess forward to offset future output VAT.

4.5 Special Sales Tax

The Special Sales Tax (SST) is a form of excise tax that applies to certain luxurious goods and selected service activities as follows:

Product	SST Rate
Cigars, cigarettes and other tobacco products	75%
Liquor and wine with ABV% ≥ 20°	65%
Liquor and wine with ABV% < 20°	35%
Beer	65%
Motor vehicles < 24 seats	10 % - 150%
Motor vehicles with cylinder capacity ≤ 2000cc	45%
Motor vehicles with cylinder capacity > 2000cc	50%
Motor vehicles with cylinder capacity > 3000cc	60%
Motorcycles with cylinder capacity > 125cc	20%
Aircraft	30%
Yachts and boats	30%
Gasoline / E5 / E10	10% / 8% / 7%
Air conditioners ≤ 90.000 BTU	10%
Playing cards	40%
Votive gift papers and objects	70%
Service	
Discotheques and dance halls	40%
Massage parlors and karaoke establishments	30%
Casino, jackpot and price-winning video games	35%
Entertainment with betting	30%
Golf	20%
Lottery	15%

The taxable price of imported goods upon importation is the dutiable price plus import duties. Taxpayers producing SST subjected goods with SST subjected raw materials are entitled to claim a credit for the SST paid on raw materials imported or purchased from domestic manufacturers. Where taxpayers pay SST at both the import and selling stages, the SST paid at importation is creditable against SST paid at the selling stage.

4.6 Import Duties

Most goods imported into Vietnam are subject to import duty which is calculated by multiplying the goods' dutiable value with the applicable import duty rate. The dutiable value of imported goods is typically based on the transaction value (i.e., the price paid or payable for the imported goods, and where appropriate, adjusted for certain dutiable or non-dutiable elements). Import duty rates are classified into three categories: ordinary rates, preferential rates, and special preferential rates. Preferential rates are applicable to imported goods from countries that have most-favoured-nation (MFN) status with Vietnam. The MFN rates are in line with Vietnam's WTO commitments and are applicable to goods imported from other WTO member countries. Special preferential rates are applicable to imported goods from countries that have a special preferential agreement or a free trade agreement with Vietnam.

To be eligible for preferential rates or special preferential rates, the imported goods must have a certificate of origin. If goods are sourced from non-preferential treatment/non-favoured countries, the ordinary rate is charged at MFN rate plus 50% surcharge. Import VAT is added in addition at a rate of usually 10%. In addition to import duty and import VAT, SST, environment protection tax, anti-dumping tax, safeguard tax and anti-subsidy tax may be applied to a number of imported goods. The customs authorities perform regular customs audits which usually focus on matters such as e.g., accurate HS code classification and goods valuation, compliance with requirements for duty exemptions and origin of goods. Import duty exemptions include:

- Machinery & equipment, specialised means of transportation and construction materials which cannot be produced in Vietnam, certain fixed assets of encouraged investment projects.
- Machinery, equipment, specialised means of transportation, materials (which cannot be produced in Vietnam), office equipment imported for use in oil and gas activities.
- Materials, supplies and components imported for the production of exported goods and materials, supplies, components imported for processing of exports.
- Goods manufactured, processed, recycled, assembled in a free trade zone without using imported raw materials or components when imported into the domestic market.
- Materials, supplies and components which cannot be domestically produced and which are imported for the production of certain encouraged projects.
- Goods temporarily imported or exported for the purpose of warranty, repair, and replacement.

A refund of import duties is only possible for: i) Goods for which import duties have been paid but which are not actually physically imported, ii) imported goods that are not used and which must be re-exported, and iii) imported materials imported for the production of goods for the domestic market but that are later used for the processing of goods for export under contracts with foreign parties.

4.7 Personal Income Tax

4.7.1 Scope and Rates

Tax residents are subject to PIT on their worldwide taxable income, wherever it is paid or received. Tax residents are individuals:

- residing in Vietnam for 183 days or more in either the calendar year or the period of 12 consecutive months from the date of first arrival, or
- having a permanent residence in Vietnam (including a registered residence which is recorded on the temporary residence card in case of foreigners, or
- having leased a property in Vietnam for at least 183 days in a tax year and unable to prove tax residence in another country.

For tax residents, the following PIT Rates apply:

Monthly Taxable Income (Million VND)	PIT Rate
➢ 0 – 5	5%
➢ 5 – 10	10%
➢ 10 – 18	15%
➢ 18 – 32	20%
➢ 32 – 52	25%
➢ 52 – 80	30%
➢ 80	35%

Tax non-residents are subject to PIT at a flat tax rate of 20% on their Vietnam related employment income, and at various other rates on their non-employment income. Individuals not meeting the conditions for being tax resident are considered tax non-residents.

4.7.2 Employment Income

Employment income is subject to PIT and includes all cash remuneration and benefits-in-kind, such as salaries, allowances, bonuses, housing- and other fringe benefits of employment paid for by the employer, including shares and other forms of company participation provided to employees. However, employment Income does not include:

- Payments for business trips, mobile phone and stationery.
- Office clothes.
- Payment for overtime (however the overtime premium only).
- Certain other collective benefits in kind such as membership fees, entertainment, healthcare, transportation to and from work, mid-shift meals.
- One-off relocation allowance to Vietnam for expatriates and from Vietnam for Vietnamese working overseas.
- School- and kindergarten fees up to high school in Vietnam for children of expatriates working in Vietnam.
- Annual return trip airfare for expatriates and Vietnamese working overseas.
- Allowances for weddings and funerals (subject to a cap).

Tax-deductible items include:

- Contributions to certain approved charities.
- Contributions to mandatory social, health and unemployment insurance schemes and contributions to local voluntary pension schemes (subject to cap).
- A personal allowance of VND 11 million per month and a dependent allowance of VND 4.4 million per month per dependent. The dependent allowance is not automatically granted; the taxpayer needs to register qualifying dependents and provide supporting documents to the tax authority (usually passports).

4.7.3 Non-Employment Income

Non-employment income includes:

Business income (including rental income): Any income derived from production and business activities as well as income from independent practice. Various flat rates apply, ranging between 0.5% - 5%, based on the type of business income. Business losses cannot be offset against employment income if an individual has income from both business and employment.

Capital investment income: Any income earned from investing in shares, making capital contributions and lending money. Types of income from capital investment include dividends and profit shares of any kind, interest on capital deposits, bonds, securities, loan interest and similar types of income. Income from capital investment is generally taxed at a flat rate of 5% (e.g., dividends and interest income, except for bank interest).

Real estate income: Income from the sale and transfer of real estate is taxed at 2% of the sales (for both residents and non-residents).

Income from franchising: Any income exceeding VND 10 million, derived by an individual from a franchising contract under which the franchisor authorizes the franchisee to purchase / sell goods or provide services in accordance with conditions imposed by the franchisor is taxed at 5%.

Income from winnings or prizes: Income from winnings or prizes in cash or in kind in excess of VND 10 million from lotteries, betting, casinos, promotional prizes and similar items is taxed at a flat rate of 10%.

Income from inheritances or gifts: Income from the receipt of inheritances or gifts in excess of VND 10 million, including securities, contributed capital, real property and other assets required to be registered is taxed at a flat rate of 10%.

Income from royalties: Any income derived from the assignment or transfer of the right to use intellectual property rights or objects including literary, artistic and scientific works, copyrights, inventions, industrial designs, trademarks, technical know-how and similar items in excess of VND 10 million (determined each time the royalties are paid) is taxed at 5%.

4.7.4 Non-Taxable Income

The following employment is not subject to PIT:

- Interest on deposits with banks and on life insurance policies.
- Compensation paid under life/ non-life insurance policies.
- Retirement pensions paid under the Social Insurance law (or the foreign equivalent).
- Income from transfer of properties between various direct family members.
- Inheritances/ gifts between various direct family members.
- Monthly retirement pensions paid under voluntary insurance schemes.
- Income of Vietnamese vessel crew members working for foreign or Vietnamese international shipping companies.
- Income from winnings at casinos.

4.7.5 Administration

The PIT year is the calendar year. However, where in the calendar year of first arrival an individual is present in Vietnam for less than 183 days, his/her first tax year is the 12-month period from the date of arrival. Subsequently, the tax year is the calendar year. All individuals with taxable income must obtain a tax code and submit their tax registration file to their employer who will subsequently submit this to the local tax office. Those who have other items of taxable income are required to submit their tax registration file to the district tax office of the locality where they reside. Regarding tax declarations, the following applies:

Employment income: For employment income, tax has to be declared and paid provisionally on a monthly basis by the 20th day of the following month or on a quarterly basis by the 30th day following the reporting quarter. The amounts paid are reconciled to the total tax liability at the year-end. An annual final tax return must be submitted and any additional tax must be paid within 90 days of the year end. Expatriate employees are also required to carry out a PIT finalization on termination of their Vietnamese assignments. Tax refunds due to excess tax payments are only available to those who have a tax code.

Non-employment income: The individual is required to declare and pay PIT in relation to each type of taxable non-employment income. The PIT regulations require income to be declared and tax paid on a receipt basis (except rental income which can be declared and tax can be paid on an annual basis). For non-employment income, PIT must be declared and paid in relation to each type of taxable non-employment income. If an individual has both business and employment income, only business income must be reported in that declaration.

Overseas income: A resident individual receiving employment income paid from overseas must also file tax declarations in Vietnam. Other types of income (capital investment, capital transfer, transfer of real property, royalties, franchising, winnings, inheritances and gifts) must be declared within ten 10 days after the date the income arises or is received. PIT paid in a foreign country on the foreign income is generally creditable under applicable DTAs.

5. Employment

5.1 Types and Content

The Vietnamese Labour Code No. 45/2019/QH14 and its implementing Decree No. 145/2020/ND-CP (Decree 145), govern employment matters in Vietnam. The VLC defines an employment contract as any "*agreement between an employee and an employer on a paid job, salary, working conditions, and the rights and obligations of each party in the labour relations.*", regardless of whether the document is called "employment contract" or not. Before recruiting an employee, an employer must conclude an employment contract in writing, except for employment for less than one month.

5.1.1 Types of Employment Contracts

Indefinite- and fixed term employment contracts: Art. 20 VLC distinguishes two types of employment contracts: Indefinite-term employment contracts and fixed-term (definite-term) employment contracts with a duration of up to 36 months. If an employee keeps working upon expiry of a fixed-term employment contract, within 30 days from the expiration date, the employer may either conclude a new employment contract or finalize the employee's leaving the company. Until such time, the parties' rights, obligations and interests specified in the old employment contract shall remain effective. If a new employment contract is not concluded after the 30-day period, the existing fixed-term employment contract shall become an indefinite employment contract. In practice, it is therefore essential that the employer does not passively tolerate the employee's continuous working after expiration but notifies the employee about either conclusion of a new employment contract or the fact that no additional employment contract will be concluded.

Number of permitted fixed-term employment contracts: Employers, after the first fixed-term employment contract expires, can only enter into ***one*** more fixed-term employment contract, and the third employment contract must then always be indefinite-term. However, employers often argue that this rule does not apply to foreign employees, as the duration of their work permit is limited to two (2) years and Art. 34 (12) VLC in addition stipulates that employment contracts automatically end if the foreign employee's work permit expires. On the other hand, work permits can be extended before they expire, and if work permits are not extended, employment agreements may also contain an extraordinary termination right for such case. Therefore, one could also well argue that the rule of having only up to two definite-term contracts applies to both Vietnamese and foreign employees. If an employer, despite the above, still wants to enter into more than two fixed-term contracts, it is therefore recommended that the employment contract then contains at least a "severability clause" stating that: *"If a provision of this employment contract is held to be illegal, invalid or unenforceable, in whole or in part, the Employer and Employee intend that the legality, validity and enforceability of the remainder of this Contract remains unaffected."*

5.1.2 Probation

Under Art. 24 VLC, the parties may either include the probation time in the employment contract or enter into a separate probation contract (except for employment contracts with a duration of less than one month). For higher-qualified jobs (especially in foreign-invested enterprises) separate probation contracts are the exception and the probationary period will be included in the employment contract. Art. 25 VLC provides that the probationary period shall not exceed:

Type of Position	Maximum Probation Period
Company executives under the LOE, including Directors, General Directors, Chief Accountants and others.	**180 calendar days**
Position requiring a junior college degree or above.	**60 calendar days**
Positions requiring a secondary vocational certificate, professional secondary school; positions for technicians and other skilled employees without junior college degree.	**30 calendar days**
All other jobs.	**6 working days**

During the probationary period, either party has the right to terminate the probation- or employment contract without prior notice and compensation obligation. The probationary salary shall not be lower than 85% of the offered salary. Upon the expiry of the probationary period, the employer shall inform the employee of the probation result. If the result is satisfactory, the employer shall keep implementing the already concluded employment contract or conclude the employment contract. (i.e., replacing the separate probation contract). If the result is not satisfactory, the employer may terminate the employment- or probation contract with immediate effect.

5.1.3 Labour Contract Contents

Under Art. 21 VLD, both indefinite- and fixed-term employment contracts must include at least the following contents:

- The employer's name, address and full name and position of the person who concludes the contract on the employer's side.
- The employee's full name, date of birth, gender, residence, identity card number or passport number.
- The duration of the employment contract in case of fixed-term employment contracts.
- The job title and place of work.
- The employee's salary and (monthly) payment date; allowances and other additional payments such as e.g. bonuses.
- The schedule for salary review and promotions (note that while the salary must be reviewed regularly, the employer need not necessarily increase it automatically with such review).
- Working hours, rest periods and vacation days.
- Personal protective equipment (if applicable).
- Employer and employee responsibility for social-, health and unemployment insurance.
- Employee training and occupational skill development.

If the job is directly related to any of the employer's business secrets or technological know-how, the employer has the right to request signing of a separate confidentiality agreement, covering scope of confidentiality and consequences of violation by the employee, including contract penalties.

Beyond the above mandatory contents, the following additional employment contract provisions are recommended:

- Confidentiality clause with regard sto the Employer's IPR, trade and business secrets,
- Non-competition clause, i.e., working for or advising the employer's competitors,
- Prohibition of multiple employments with other employers (even if non-competing),
- Non-poaching of employees after termination, and
- Rules on conflict of interest and anti-corruption, ideally supported by a local "Code of Conduct" (CoC)" that covers all major compliance topics in one document.

Typical cases of non-compliance when concluding local Vietnamese employment contracts with foreigners include:

- *Supporting Expats by reducing Vietnamese PIT by splitting their worldwide income into an offshore contract (employment or consulting) and Vietnam employment, with the Vietnam employment contract stating an unusually low salary amount. While popular in the past, it is increasingly scrutinized by Vietnamese authorities in the context of tax evasion.*

- *Supporting both Expats and Vietnamese employees in reducing Vietnamese PIT by separating the Employee's allowances from his/her salary, and massively overstating the allowance amounts (housing, transportation &*

travel, food, mobile phone and other communications) in comparison to the contract salary.

- *Signing Vietnamese employment contracts not addressing or trying to avoid payment of mandatory compulsory social security and health insurance contributions.*

- *Employers failing to register their employees within 30 days of signing their employment contracts with the competent social security and health insurance agencies; not updating any employee information relating thereto. In such case, employers may be subject to penalties from the authorities in charge and also face a risk of being sued by employees.*

5.1.4 Overtime

According to Art. 105 VLC, working hours must not exceed eight hours per day or 48 hours per week. Overtime work is any work performed beyond the agreed working hours in the employee's employment contract. An employer only has the right to request an employee to work overtime if all of the following conditions are met:

- The employee agrees to work overtime.
- The total normal working hours plus overtime working hours shall not exceed 12 hours per day, and 40 hours per month.
- The total overtime working hours do not exceed 200 hours in one (1) year.

Additionally, employers may request an employee to work overtime for up to 300 hours in one (1) year in the following fields, works, jobs and cases:

- Manufacturing, processing of textiles, garments, footwear, electric (products), processing of agricultural, forestry, aquaculture products, salt production.
- Generation and supply of electricity, telecommunications, refinery operation; water supply and drainage.
- Works that require highly skilled workers that are not available on the labour market at the time.
- Urgent works that cannot be delayed due to seasonal reasons or availability of materials or products, bad weather, natural disasters, fire, hostility, shortage of power or raw materials, or technical issue of the production line.

Overtime will be paid based on the employee's salary as follows:

- On normal days: at least 150%.
- On weekly days off: at least 200%
- During public holidays and on paid leave: at least 300%, not including the daily salary during the public holidays or paid leave for employees receiving daily salaries.

An employee who works at night will be paid an additional amount of at least 30% of the normal salary. An employee who works overtime at night will be paid, in addition to the above, an amount of at least 20% of the day work salary of a normal day, weekend or public holiday.

While many employers would like to fully exclude in the employment contract the employee's right to overtime compensation, this is not generally permitted. However, an overtime clause in the employment contract may specify the requirements for overtime compensation as follows:

Overtime Clause: *"The Employee is expected to fulfil his / her tasks under this Labour Contract in his / her regular working time, and overtime should therefore generally not be re-quired. Overtime requested by the Employee in writing can only be compensated if i) the Employer approves in writing the Employee's written overtime request before the overtime occurs and ii) the Employee has worked the full number of hours per week in accordance with this Employment Contract. Overtime requests and approvals must be made monthly, within five (5) working days after the end of each calendar month. If the Employer approves the Employee's written overtime request in writing, overtime shall generally be compensated in the form of equivalent time off. Overtime compen-sation not claimed within three (3) months after the Employer's approval shall be forfeited."*

5.1.5 Leave Entitlements

An employee working for at least 12 months is entitled to minimum annual leave of 12 days (One day per month) in addition to public holidays and at least one weekly day off. The employee's annual leave entitlement must increase by at least one day for every five years of employment with the same employer. An employee who has been working for an employer for less than 12 months will have a number of paid leave days proportional to the number of working months. An employee who, due to employment termination or job loss, has not taken or not entirely taken up his/her annual leave shall be paid in compensation for the untaken leave days.

In addition, an employee is entitled to take a fully paid personal leave in the following circumstances: i) Marriage: three days, ii) Marriage of his/her biological or adopted child: one day, iii) Death of his/her biological or adoptive parent; death of his/her spouse's biological or adoptive parent; death of spouse, biological or adopted child: three days. In such cases, the employee is further entitled to take one additional day of unpaid leave and must inform the employer in case of the death of his/her grandparent or biological sibling; marriage of his/her parent or natural sibling.

Finally, employee and employer may at all times also agree on additional unpaid leave.

5.2 Employment Termination

5.2.1 Case Groups

Art. 34 VLC recognizes the following cases of employment termination:

1. The employment contract expires.
2. The tasks stated in the contract have been completed.
3. Both parties agree to terminate the employment contract.
4. The employee is sentenced to imprisonment without being eligible for suspension or release, in case of capital punishment

or the employee is prohibited from performing the work stated in the employment contract by an effective verdict or judgment of the court.

5. The foreign employee working in Vietnam is expelled by an effective verdict or judgment of the court or a decision of a competent authority.
6. The employee dies; is declared by the court as a legally incapacitated person, missing or dead.
7. The employer that is a natural person dies; is declared by the court as a legally incapacitated person, missing or dead. The employer that is not a natural person ceases to operate.
8. The employee is dismissed for disciplinary reasons.
9. The employee unilaterally terminates the employment contract.
10. The employer unilaterally terminates the employment contract.
11. The employer allows the employee to resign according to Art. 43 VLC.
12. The work permit of a foreign employee expires according to Art. 156 VLC.
13. The employee fails to perform his/her tasks during the probationary period under the employment contract or gives up the probation.

5.2.2 Unilateral Employee Termination

Termination without cause: Employees may unilaterally terminate their employment contract, provided they notify the employee in advance:

- 45 days in case of indefinite-term contracts.
- 30 days in case of fixed-term contracts of 12-36 months.
- 3 working days in case of a fixed term contracts under 12 months.

Immediate termination with cause: Employees have the right to unilaterally terminate their employment contract without prior notice if they are:

- not assigned to the work or workplace or not provided with the working conditions as agreed in the employment contract.
- not paid adequately or on schedule.
- maltreated, assaulted, physically or verbally insulted by the employer in a manner that affects the employee's health, dignity or honour or forced to work against their will.
- sexually harassed in the workplace.
- pregnant and have to stop working.
- reaching the retirement age unless otherwise agreed, or
- they find that the employer fails to provide truthful information in accordance with Art. 16 VLC in a manner affecting employment contract performance.

5.2.3 Unilateral Employer Termination

Under Art. 36 VLC, an employer has the right to unilaterally terminate an employment contract in one of the following circumstances:

a. The employee repeatedly fails to perform his/her work according to the criteria for assessment of employees' fulfilment of duties established by the employer. The criteria for assessment of employees' fulfilment of duties shall be established by the employer with consideration taken of opinions offered by the representative organization of employees (if any).

b. The employee is sick or has an accident and remains unable to work after having received treatment for a period of 12 consecutive months in the case of an indefinite-term employment contract, for 06 consecutive months in the case of an employment contract with a fixed term of 12 – 36 months, or more than half the duration of the contract in case of an employment contract with a fixed term of less than 12 months. Upon recovery, the employer may consider concluding another employment contract with the employee.

c. In the event of a natural disaster, fire, major epidemic, hostility, relocation or downsizing requested by a competent authority, the employer has to lay off employees after all possibilities have been exhausted.

d. The employee is not present at the workplace after the time limit specified in Art. 31 VLC.

e. The employee reaches the retirement age as per Art. 169 VLC.

f. The employee quits his/her fails to go to work without acceptable excuses for at least five consecutive working days.

g. The employee fails to provide truthful information during the conclusion of the employment contract in accordance with Art. 16 VLC in a manner that affects the recruitment.

When unilaterally terminating the employment contract in any of the cases specified in above points a, b, c, e and g, the employer shall inform the employer in advance:

- 45 days in case of indefinite-term contracts.
- 30 days in case of fixed-term contracts between 12 – 36 months.
- 3 working days in case of fixed-term employment of less than 12 months and in the cases stipulated in point b above.

When unilaterally terminating the employment contract in points d and f above, the employer need not inform the employee in advance. Employers must not unilaterally terminate the contract if the employee:

- is suffering from an illness or work accident, occupational disease and is being treated or nursed under the decision of a competent health institution, except the cases in Art. 36 (1b) VLC.
- is on annual, personal or any other type of permitted leave.
- is pregnant, on maternal leave or raising a child under 12 months of age.

5.2.4 Illegal Unilateral Termination

By the employee: The employee who illegally unilaterally terminates his/her employment contract shall: i) not receive the severance allowance, ii) pay the employer a compensation that is worth his/her half a month's salary plus an amount equal to his/her salary for the remaining notice period from the termination date, and iii) reimburse the employer with training costs.

By the employer: The employer that illegally unilaterally terminates an employment contract with an employee shall reinstate the employee in accordance with the original employment contract, and pay the salary, social insurance, health insurance and unemployment insurance premiums for the period during which the employee was not allowed to work, plus at least two months' salary specified in the employment contract. After the reinstatement, the employee must return the severance allowance or redundancy allowance (if any) to the employer. Where there is no longer a vacancy for the position or work as agreed in the employment contract and the employee still wishes to work, the employer shall negotiate revisions to the employment contract. In case the employee does not wish to return to work, the employer shall pay an additional severance allowance in accordance with above principles.

Where the employer does not wish to reinstate the employee and the employee agrees, both parties shall negotiate, beyond the severance payment, an additional compensation which shall be at least an additional two months' salary under the employment contract in order to terminate the employment contract.

5.2.5 Termination for Economic Reasons

Art. 42 VLC allows employers to unilaterally terminate employees in case of "changes in structure, technology or changes due to economic reasons." Changes in structure and technology include i) changes in the company's organizational structure or personnel rearrangement, ii) changes in processes, technology, equipment associated with the employer's business lines and changes in products or product structure. Changes due to economic reasons include economic crisis or economic depression and changes in law and state policies upon restructuring of the economy or implementation of international commitments. In addition, Art. 43 VLC allows employers to terminate employees in cases of restructuring such as e.g., full or partial division, consolidation, conversion, merger or sale of the enterprise.

Employers who want to terminate employees for economic reasons or due to restructuring must first implement a "labour utilization plan" if the change affects the employment of a large number of employees. In case of new vacancies, priority shall be given to retraining the existing employees. If the employer is unable to create alternative employment and is forced to terminating employees, the employer is obliged to pay redundancy allowances to the affected employees (see 5.2.6. below).

5.2.6 Severance Payments

In case an employment contract is terminated as per prescribed in above 6.2.1 No. 1, 2, 3, 4, 6, 7, 9 and 10, the employee has worked for the employer on a regular basis for at least 12 months, the employer shall pay the employee a severance allowance amounting to ***half a month's salary for each year of work***, except for the cases in which the employee is entitled to receive retirement benefits as prescribed by social insurance laws.

In case an employment contract is terminated for economic reasons or due to restructuring, and the employee has worked on a regular basis for the employer for at least 12 months, the employer shall pay a redundancy allowance amounting to ***one month's salary for each year of work***, with the total redundancy allowance being at least two month's salaries. The qualified period of work as the basis for calculation of severance or redundancy allowance is the employee's total employment time minus the period over which the employee has participated in the mandatory unemployment insurance scheme. The salary as the basis for calculation of both severance and redundancy allowance shall be the average contract salary of the last six months prior to termination.

5.3 Internal Labour Regulations

5.3.1 Minimum Content

According to Art. 118 VLC, every employer with at least 10 employees must have Internal Labour Regulations (ILRs) and register these at their local Department of Labour, Invalids and Social Affairs (DOLISA).

The ILRs must include at least the following provisions:

- Working hours and rest periods.

- Order at the workplace.
- Occupational safety and health.
- Actions against sexual harassment in the workplace.
- Protection of employer's assets, business secrets and intellectual property.
- Cases in which reassignment of employees are permitted.
- Violations against the ILRs and disciplinary measures.
- Material responsibility for damages.
- Authorized person(s) to take disciplinary measures.

Once issued, the employees must be notified of the ILRs by displaying them at the workplace and/or in the company's Intranet.

5.3.2 Labour Discipline

The employee's violation of the ILRs authorizes the employer, under the requirements laid out in the ILRs, to i) reprimand the employee, ii) defer a due salary raise for up to 6 months, iii) demote the employee or iv) dismiss the employee. Art. 125 VLC allows dismissal in the following cases:

- The employee commits an act of theft, embezzlement, gambling, deliberately inflicts injuries or uses drug at work.
- The employee discloses technological or business secrets or infringes the intellectual property rights of the employer.

- The employee commits acts which are seriously detrimental or are posing a seriously detrimental threat to the assets or interests of the employer.

- The employee commits sexual harassment in the workplace.

- The employee repeats a violation which was priorly disciplined by deferment of salary raise or demotion and has not been absolved. A repeated violation means a violation which was disciplined and is repeated before it is absolved in accordance with Art. 126 VLC (according to which an employee who is disciplined by reprimand, deferment of salary raise or demotion will have the previous violation absolved after three months, six months or three years respectively from the day on which the disciplinary measure is imposed if he/she does not commit any other violation against the ILRs).

- The employee fails to go to work for a total period of five days in 30 days, or for a total period of 20 days in 365 days from the first day he/she fails to go to work without acceptable excuses. Justified reasons include natural disasters;; the employee or his/her family member suffers from illness if certified by a health facility; and other reasons as stipulated in the ILRs.

When imposing disciplinary measures, employers must not:

- Harm the employee's health, life, honour or dignity.

- Apply monetary fines or deducting amounts from the employee's salary.

- Impose a disciplinary measure against an employee for a violation which is not stipulated in the ILRs, the employee's employment contract or the VLC.

5.3.3 Work suspension

An employer has the right to suspend an employee if an alleged violation of the employment contract, the ILRs or the VLC is of a complicated nature and where the continued presence of the employee at the workplace is deemed to cause difficulties for the investigation. However, an employee can only be suspended from work after consultation with the representative organization of the employees.

The suspension shall not exceed 15 days, or 90 days in special circumstances. During the suspension, the employee shall receive an advance of 50% of his/her salary. Upon the expiry of the work suspension, the employer shall reinstate the employee. Where the employee is disciplined, he/she shall not be required to return the advanced salary. If the employee is not disciplined, he/she is entitled to full salary for the suspension period.

5.3.4 Procedural requirements

Disciplinary measures against an employee require the following:

- The employer is able to prove the employee's fault.
- A representative organization of employees to which the employee is a member participates in the procedure.

- The employee is physically present and has the right to defend him/herself, request a lawyer or the representative organization of employees to defend him/her; if the employee is under 15 years , parent or a legal representative must be present.
- The disciplinary process is recorded in writing.

In practice, dismissal of employees is not easy: *It requires the Employer to evidence the employee's fault, for example by providing written state-ments of witnesses, and a prior written warning letter to the employee stat-ing exactly when he / she has committed each violation of the ILRs (with signature/stamp of the employer, to be acknowledged by the employee). Warning emails are insufficient and it is therefore crucial to have two warning letters, with the first letter setting a deadline for the employee to correct his/her wrong behaviour or actions.*

It is prohibited to impose more than one disciplinary measure for one violation of the ILRs. Where an employee commits multiple violations of the ILRs, he/she shall be subjected to the heaviest disciplinary measure for the most serious violation. In addition, no disciplinary measure shall be taken against an employee if the employee is:

- taking leave on account of illness or convalescence or on other types of leave with the employer's consent.
- being held under temporary custody or detention.
- waiting for verification and conclusion of the competent agency for violations.

- pregnant, on maternal leave or raising a child under 12 months.
- suffering from a mental illness or another disease which causes the loss of consciousness or the loss of his/her behavioural control when violating the ILRs.

The time limit for disciplinary measures against an ILR violation is six months from the date of the violation and 12 months for violations relating to finance, assets and disclosure of technological or business secrets.

5.3.5 Labour Dispute Settlement

Article 187 VLC provides the following competences:

Settlement by labour mediators: Individual labour disputes shall generally be settled through mediation by labour mediators before being brought to the Labour Arbitration Council (LAC) or the competent court, except for the following labour disputes for which mediation is not mandatory (amongst others): Disputes over dismissal and unilateral termination of employment contracts, disputes over damages and/or allowances upon termination of employment contracts, disputes over social-, health or unemployment insurance. The time limit to request a labour mediator to settle an individual labour dispute is six (6) months from the date on which a party discovers the act of infringement of their lawful rights and interests.

Settlement by Labour Arbitration Council: The parties may, by consensus, request the LAC to settle a dispute if mediation is not mandatory. Within 30 working days from establishment of the arbitral tribunal, it shall issue a decision on the settlement of the labour dispute. In case an arbitral tribunal is not established by the deadline, a decision on the settlement of the labour dispute is not issued by the deadline or a disputing party fails to comply with the decision of the arbitral tribunal, the parties are entitled to bring the case to People's Court. The time limit to request the LAC to settle an individual labour dispute is nine (9) months from the date on which a party discovers the violation of their rights, interests or applicable laws.

Settlement by the People's Court: The parties are generally entitled to request the People's Court to settle the case if mediation is not mandatory and/or arbitration is not agreed on. The time limit to bring an individual labour dispute to the People's Court is one (1) year from the day on which a party discovers the violation of their rights, interests or applicable laws.

5.4 Labour Outsourcing

Labour outsourcing means that an employee enters into an employment contract with an outsourcing agency, which subsequently outsources its employee to work for a client enterprise. Labour outsourcing is a conditional business, requires a labour outsourcing license, is permitted for up to 12 months and only for certain types of work as follows:

- The employment is necessary for the sharp increase in labour demand over a limited period of time.
- The outsourced employee replaces another employee who is taking maternal leave, has an occupational accident or occupational disease or has to fulfil his/her citizen's duties.

- The work requires highly skilled workers.

The client enterprise may not employ an outsourced employee if:

- The outsourced employee is meant to replace another employee during a strike or settlement of labour disputes;
- There is no agreement with the outsourcing agency on responsibility for compensation for the outsourced employee's occupational accidents and diseases;
- The outsourced employee is meant to replace another employee who is dismissed due to changes in organizational structure, technology, economic reasons, full division, partial division, consolidation or merger of the enterprise.

The client enterprise must not outsource an outsourced employee to another employer and must not employ an employee outsourced by an agency that does not have a valid labour outsourcing license. The outsourcing agency and the client enterprise's labour outsourcing contract must contain the following:

- The work location, the vacancy to be filled by the outsourced employee, detailed description of the work, and detailed requirements for the outsourced employee;
- The labour outsourcing duration; the starting date of the outsourcing period;
- Working hours, rest periods, occupational safety and health at the workplace;

- Compensation responsibility in case of occupational accidents and diseases;
- Obligations of each party to the outsourced employee.

The labour outsourcing contract must not include any agreement on employee rights and benefits less favourable than those in the employment contract between the employee and the outsourcing agency.

Rights and obligations of the outsourcing agency:

- Provide an outsourced employee who meets the requirements of the client enterprise and the employment contract signed with the employee;
- Inform the outsourced employee of the content of the outsourcing contract;
- Provide the client enterprise with the curriculum vitae of the outsourced employee, and his/her requirements.
- Pay the outsourced employee a salary that is not lower than that of a directly hired employee of the client enterprise who has equal qualifications and performs the same or equal work;
- Keep records of the number of outsourced employees, the client enterprise, submit periodic reports to the labour authority.
- Take disciplinary measures against the outsourced employee if the client enterprise returns the employee for violations against labour regulations.

Rights and obligations of the client enterprise:

- Inform and guide the outsourced employee about its ILRs and other regulations.
- Not to discriminate between the outsourced employee and its directly hired employees in respect of the working conditions.
- Reach an agreement with the outsourced employee on night work and overtime work in accordance with the VLC.
- The client enterprise may negotiate with the outsourced employee and the outsourcing agency official employment of the outsourced employee while the employment contract between the outsourced employee and the outsourcing agency is still unexpired.
- Return the outsourced employee who does not meet agreed conditions or violates rules of the outsourcing enterprise.
- Provide evidence of violations against work regulations by the outsourced employee to the outsourcing agency for disciplinary measures.

Rights and obligations of the outsourced employee:

- Perform the work in accordance with the employment contract with the outsourcing agency;
- Obey ILRs, management, administration and supervision by client enterprise;

- Receive a salary which is not lower than that of a directly hired employee of the client enterprise with equal qualifications and performing the same or equal job;
- File a complaint with the outsourcing enterprise in case the client enterprise violates the labour outsourcing contract.
- Negotiate termination of the employment contract with the outsourcing agency in order to conclude an employment contract with the client enterprise.

5.5 Social Security Obligations

While social insurance (SI) and health insurance (HI) contributions are mandatory for both foreign and Vietnamese employees, unemployment insurance (UI) contributions are mandatory for Vietnamese employees only.

Statutory employer contributions do not constitute a taxable benefit to the employee; however, the employee's contributions are PIT deductible. SI/HI/UI contributions are based on the employees' monthly gross income (salary, allowances and other regular payments).

Health- and social insurance contributions: Both Vietnamese and foreigners employed in Vietnam for three (3) months or more are subject to compulsory HI contributions. In addition, since January 2022, both Vietnamese and foreigners employed in Vietnam for 12 months or more are also subject to compulsory social insurance contributions, in which employers are obliged to contribute from the employee's gross salary 3% to the "sickness and maternity fund", 0.5% to the "occupational accidents and occupational diseases fund" and 14% to the "retirement and death fund" (total 17.5%). The employee contributes 8% only to the retirement and death fund. The maximum monthly salary that is subject to SI/HI contributions is capped at 29,800,000 VND, being 20 times the ***minimum basic wage*** (applicable to public sector employees, currently VND 1,490,000 VND per month).

Unemployment insurance contributions: Unemployment insurance compensates Vietnamese employees for job loss or termination. Employer and employee will each contribute to the UI 1% of the employee's gross salary, up to 20 times the ***minimum regional salary*** (which applies to non-public sector employees). The government distinguishes four zones to determine the minimum regional salary. Per 1st July 2022, the following applies:

- ***Zone 1:*** VND 4,680,000 (approximately USD 200) - Hanoi and Ho Chi Minh City urban areas and certain neighbouring industrial areas in Binh Duong and Dong Nai.
- ***Zone 2:*** VND 4,160,000 (approximately USD 179) - Hanoi and Ho Chi Minh City rural areas and other major urban areas such as Can Tho, Danang and Hai Phong.
- ***Zone 3:*** VND 3,640,000 (approximately USD 156) - Provincial cities and the districts of Bac Ninh, Bac Giang and Hai Duong.
- ***Zone 4:*** VND 3,250,000 (approximately USD 140) – Rural Areas and rest of Vietnam.

In summary, the following contribution requirements apply:

Contribution Type	Employer	Employee
Social Insurance *Vietnamese and foreigners*	Sickness and maternity fund: 3% Occupational disease and accident fund: 0.5% Retirement and death fund: 14%	N/A N/A 8%
Health Insurance *Vietnamese and foreigners*	3%	1.5%
Unemployment Insurance *Vietnamese nationals only*	1%	1%
Total	**21.5%**	**10.5%**

Statutory retirement / pension benefits: Any employee, including foreign employees, will receive a retirement pension if

- He/she has paid social insurance for at least 20 years and
- He/she has reached the retirement age specified in Art. 169 (2) VLC, according to which "*Retirement ages of employees in normal working conditions shall be gradually increased to 62 for males by 2028 and 60 for females in 2035.*" Since 2023, the retirement ages of employees are 60 years and nine months for males and 56 years for females, and it will annually increase by three / four months for males/ females.

If you qualify, you will receive a pension equal to 45% of the monthly salary on which your social insurance contributions were based. Note that the maximum monthly salary that is subject to SI/HI contributions is capped at 29,800,000 VND, being 20 times the minimum basic wage (applicable to public sector employees, currently VND 1,490,000 VND per month).Therefore, your pension would then be 45% of the 29.8 million VND per month Vietnamese and foreign employees who have paid social insurance for a period of time as prescribed by social insurance laws shall receive a retirement pension when he/she reaches the retirement age.

The retirement ages of employees in normal working conditions will be gradually increased to 62 for males by 2028 and 60 for females in 2035. Since 2021, the retirement ages of employees are 60 years and three months for males and 55 years and four months for females, and it annually increases by three / four months for males/ females.

5.6 Local Employment of Foreigners

The local employment of foreigners in Vietnam is governed by the VLC and Decree No. 152/2020/ND-CP on "*Foreign workers working in Vietnam and Recruitment and Management of Vietnamese workers working for foreign employers in Vietnam*" (Decree 152). According to Art. 152 VLC, foreigners should only be employed in Vietnam to hold highly qualified positions of e.g., managers, executives, specialists and technical workers/engineers and if professional requirements for those cannot be met by Vietnamese employees.

Prior to hiring foreign employees, employers must therefore file an annual report of demand on their use of foreign employees to the local DOLISA for approval by the People's Committee, and an application for a work permit cannot be processed until obtaining this approval. Vietnamese authorities are increasingly enforcing violations and employees working in Vietnam without a work permit may be penalized or, if unable to meet work permit requirements, deported back to their home countries within 15 days. In addition, the employer's operations may be suspended for up to three months with a possible penalty of up to 75 million VND.

5.6.1 Work Permit

Art. 153 VLC states that unless an exemption applies, all foreign nationals who want to work in Vietnam must obtain a work permit. Employing foreign nationals without a valid work permit is subject to penalties and sanctions. Art. 154 VLC and Art. 7 of Decree 152 detail that a foreigner working in Vietnam is exempt from the work permit requirement if he/she

- is the owner or ahareholder of a limited liability company with a capital contribution value of at least 3 billion VND.
- is the Chairperson or a member of the Board of Directors of a joint-stock company with a capital contribution value of at least 3 billion VND.
- is an intra-company transferee within 11 sectors in the schedule of commitments in services between Vietnam and the WTO, including: business services, communication services, construction services, distribution services, educational services, environmental services, financial services, health services, tourism services, recreational and cultural services and transport services.

- is the manager of a representative office, project or the person in charge of the operation of an international organization or a foreign non-governmental organization in Vietnam.
- enters Vietnam for a period of less than 3 months to do marketing of a service.
- enters Vietnam for a period of less than 3 months to a resolve complicated technical or technological issue which (i) affects or threatens to affect business operation and (ii) cannot be resolved by Vietnamese experts or any other foreign experts currently in Vietnam.
- is a foreign lawyer who has been granted a lawyer's practising certificate in Vietnam in accordance with the Law on Lawyers.
- is granted a communication and journalism practicing certificate in Vietnam by the Ministry of Foreign Affairs.
- is one of the cases specified in an international treaty to which the Socialist Republic of Vietnam is a signatory applies.
- enters Vietnam to provide professional and engineering consulting services or perform other tasks intended for research, formulation, appraisal, supervision, evaluation, management and execution of programs and projects using official development assistance (ODA) in accordance with regulations or agreement in international treaties on ODA signed between the competent authorities of Vietnam and foreign countries.

- is sent by a foreign competent authority or organization to Vietnam to teach and study at an international school under management of a foreign diplomatic mission or the United Nations; or of a facility established under an agreement to which Vietnam is a signatory.
- is a volunteer as specified in Art. 3 of Decree 152.
- enters Vietnam to hold the position of a manager, executive, expert or technical worker for a period of work of less than 30 days and up to 3 times a year.
- enters Vietnam to implement an international agreement to which a central or provincial authority is a signatory.
- is a student studying at a foreign school or training institution which has a probation agreement with an agency, organization or enterprise in Vietnam; or a probationer or apprentice on a Vietnam sea-going ship.
- is a relative of a member of foreign representative body in Vietnam as specified in Art. 2 of Decree 152.
- obtains an official passport to work for a regulatory agency, political organization, or socio-political organization.
- takes charge of establishing a commercial presence.
- is certified by the Ministry of Education and Training as a foreign worker entering Vietnam for teaching and research purpose.

Despite being exempted by law from the work permit requirement, foreigners falling under one of the above exemptions still need a "*certification of exemption from work permit*" which is granted by the DOLISA of the province where the foreign worker is expected to work. The employer shall request the DOLISA to certify that such foreign worker is eligible for exemption from a work permit at least 10 working days before he/she starts to work. The validity period of a certification of exemption from work permit is up to 2 years. If a certification of exemption from work permit is re-issued, the corresponding validity period is up to 2 years.

5.6.2 Application

If a work permit must be obtained, the application process is supposed to only take 15 working days but may take longer in practice. Therefore, companies planning to employ a non-exempted employee in Vietnam should apply for the work permit 2-3 weeks prior to the foreign employee's intended contract start date. To apply for a work permit, the foreign employee must provide the employer with the following documents:

- Legalized copy of their passport,
- "Fitness to work certificate" issued by a foreign or Vietnamese competent health facility issued within 12 months before the submission date of the application,
- Legalized police (clearance) certificate issued by a foreign or Vietnamese authority issued within six months before the submission date of the application.

- Proof as a manager, executive or expert (such as university degree or evidence of relevant experience, curriculum vitae).
- Two colour photos (4cm x 6cm size), taken within 6 months before application.
- An acceptance of demand for foreign workers.

After initial approval, a work permit is valid for a maximum of two (2) years and can be extended in a procedure similar to obtaining the original work permit.

A work permit is or becomes invalid if:

- The employment contract is terminated and/or the contents of the employment contract are inconsistent with the contents of the work permit granted.
- The work performed does not conform with the contents of the work permit.
- The contract on which the work permit was granted expires or is terminated.
- The foreign party issues a written notice which terminates the outsourcing of the foreign employee to Vietnam.
- The Vietnamese party or foreign organization that hires the foreign employee ceases its operation.
- The work permit is revoked.

5.7 Practical Tips

5.7.1 Tips for Expat Assignments

In case of expatriate employees (expats) transferred by their overseas employer to Vietnam, the local Vietnamese employment contract will often not be the only relevant legal document with regards to the expat's employment in Vietnam (from the foreign company's point of view). Rather, an assignment contract and / or an overseas employment contract (active or "dormant") will often complement the local Vietnamese employment.

As the Vietnamese local employment contract, assignment contract and the applicable law may conflict, the following aspects should be considered when negotiating expat assignments:

- ***Conclude a local employment contract:*** In some cases, employers will try to not even conclude a local Vietnamese employment contract for the assignment time to Vietnam but comply with their Vietnamese legal obligations by providing to the authorities a translation of the overseas assignment contract only. While this is legally possible, it may create uncertainties for both the Expat and the Employer for example with regards to minimum Vietnamese legal requirements. It is therefore recommended to conclude for every assignment to Vietnam a Vietnamese local employment contract to supplement the Expat's overseas and/or assignment contract to Vietnam.

- *Return clauses or reinstatement guarantee:* If the employer wishes to cancel the overseas employment contract and replace it only with a local Vietnamese employment contract, the Expat should consider requesting at least a "return clause" or "reinstatement guarantee" in addition to the local employment contract. More favourable for the Expat is an assignment contract according to which the overseas contract is not cancelled but set as "dormant" for the duration of the assignment and then automatically "revives" once the assignment is completed.
- *Consider "dual" termination protection:* With regards to employment termination, the best-case for the Expat (and worst-case for the employer) is where two valid employment contracts exist: A local Vietnamese employment contract and in addition, a (dormant) overseas employment contract with an assignment component or assignment contract that connects both contracts. In such case, to fire the employee, employers must subsequently terminate first the local Vietnamese employment contract and then the ("revived") overseas employment contract, thereby doubling their efforts and risks.
- *Agree on allocation of local social insurance contributions:* As Expats will be subject to mandatory Vietnamese social security and PIT obligations for the time of their assignment, the assignment contract should address precisely who will pay the ongoing overseas social security obligations during the time of the assignment. The same is true for the Expat's accumulation

of overseas pension benefits and contributions to respective mandatory or voluntary pension funds overseas. With regards to the Expat's potentially additional PIT burden resulting from the assignment to Vietnam, the assignment contract may either include a "net-salary clause" or a "tax- equalization" clause stating that the employer must burden or neutralize any PIT disadvantages resulting from the assignment.

- ***Accumulation of severance payments in subsequent expats postings:*** With regards to severance payments in the event of termination of the Expat's employment during the assignment abroad, some employers try to limit their severance obligations to the time of the assignment according to local Vietnamese law and ignore the Expat's overall employment time with the global employer. Therefore, a "severance clause" in the (active or dormant) overseas contract should clearly address the Expat's entry date to the company headquarters / company group and stipulate clearly that severance entitlements apply for the entire time period from the entry date to the termination date (regardless of where the employment was terminated). In addition, it should be stipulated which severance amount and calculation should apply under which applicable law (e.g., headquarters or assignment location or combined).
- ***Check relocation clauses carefully:*** Employers usually aim at a high degree of flexibility with regards to Expat relocation and phrase relocation- / transfer clauses broadly. Expats should

therefore carefully look at the wording of such clauses to avoid the uncertainty to be transferred at any time to any location. At least, some objective criteria should be established according to which the employer may relocate the employee (such as e.g., comparability of new location in terms of both job requirements and environment).

- *Agree on applicable law for all employment contracts:* Regarding the applicable law, some employers like to exclude in the assignment contract or the local employment contract the application of Vietnamese labour laws even though Vietnamese law is territorially applicable. It should be clearly defined here that the employer does not have such "cherry-picking" right. Rather, in cases of conflict between Vietnamese and overseas laws, the more favourable law for the Expat should apply.

5.7.2 Other Do's and Don'ts

- *Don't rely on CV information alone:* Next to CVs, you also ask for copies of candidate's academic records (such as, e.g., university degrees, English tests etc.). In addition, candidates should provide reference letters and reference contacts to allow you to call former employers directly. While reference letters are generally phrased too well-meaning, only a direct call with (former) employer(s) may generate more candid statements about the candidate's actual skills in reality.

- *Use recruiters for pre-selection:* The pre-selection process saves you time and may include initial interviews and certain tests to validate the candidate's skills, qualifications and experience. Also, recruiters can pre-select based on the candidate's salary expectation and check the candidate's motives. However, while the use of recruiters is useful, employers should not limit their pre-selection to just a few final candidates but request at least 10-15 CVs to get a better idea of who is available in the market.

- *Don't hire "friends and family":* It is generally recommended to dismiss recommendations of "friends and family" by existing company staff to avoid conflict of interest at the workplace in principle. If, exceptionally, such recommendations are considered, a careful and thorough background screening of such candidates should be conducted. If such screening reveals even the slightest doubt, the candidate should not be hired simply to avoid the mere impression of favourism.

- *Make professional and compliant Vietnamese employment contracts:* Employers should make sure the employment contract contains at least the legal minimum requirements and is made in Vietnamese language. In addition, include employer-protective clauses such as provisions on confidentiality, non-competition, non-poaching, rules on conflict of interest and anti-corruption.

- *Understand local salary standards:* Employers should have a salary range for their positions, based on competitive market rates. If candidates ask for less than market standard despite formally meeting qualifications, they may not be seriously interested in the job and have other motives instead (for example, setting-up or already running their own side business)

- *Include job description and targets in employment contracts:* Clearly agree on the standards for the employee's expected performance to make it easier for the company to terminate the employee for non-performance. If no job description and no key performance indicators and performance requirements are agreed upon in writing (by annexing both to the employment contract), Vietnamese courts will generally argue that employees are not obliged to deliver specific results but only offer their work as specified in the employment contract.
- *Don't enter into indefinite employment contracts right away:* Employers should always enter into a fixed-term employment contract (usually 12-24 months for first time employment) rather than signing an indefinite-term employment contract right away. This, in combination with the probation period, gives employers more flexibility to easily dispose of employees not fit for the job by simply letting the contract expire.
- *Include a probation time in the employment contract:* A probation time should be agreed with all candidates. The probation time can be up to 180 days for executive positions. This gives employers sufficient time to assess the candidate "on the job" and terminate the employment after unsuccessful probation.

- ***Have Internal Labour Regulations (ILRs) registered with the DOLISA:*** In addition to job description and performance targets, the ILRs allow you to define in great detail the requirements for sanctioning an employee's violation of company rules and other misconduct. The ILRs will make it easier for you to terminate an employee who violates laws, regulations and internal rules.

- ***Limit signing authority of executives:*** If you hire General Directors or other executives, make sure that their signing authority for business and financial transactions is limited or controlled. This is particularly true if those executives are appointed as Legal Representatives of your company at the same time. Regarding bank transactions, register with the bank the persons allowed to transact, alone or together, up to which amounts.

6. Intellectual Property Rights

6.1 Classification

Intellectual property rights (IPRs) are governed by Vietnam's Law on Intellectual Property No. 50/2005/QH11, which was amended and further supplemented in 2019 (IP Law). Vietnam's legal framework for the protection of IPRs is relatively comprehensive, covering most aspects of IPR protection in accordance with international standards. The IP Law regulates the following IPRs:

- ***Industrial property rights:*** comprise inventions, industrial designs, designs of semi-conducting closed circuits, trade secrets, marks, trade names and geographical indications.
- ***Copyrights:*** comprise literary, artistic and scientific works; the subject matter of copyright related rights shall comprise performances, audio and visual fixation, broadcasts and satellite signals carrying coded programmes.
- ***Rights to plant varieties:*** comprises plant varieties and reproductive materials.

Vietnam is a member to numerous international conventions regulating IPRs, amongst others: the Agreement on Trade-Related Aspects of International Property Rights (TRIPS), the Berne Convention, the Paris Convention for the Protection of Industrial Property, the Madrid Agreement concerning the International Registration of Marks, the Rome Convention for the Protection of Performers, the Producers of Phonograms and

Broadcasting Organizations, the Patent Cooperation Treaty and the International Convention for the Protection of New Varieties of Plants. Since December 30th December 2019, European companies and designers are also able to use the Hague System to protect their industrial designs in Vietnam.

IPRs can be either registered or unregistered: Unregistered IPRs automatically give their owner legal title to their creation, such as e.g., copyrights, unregistered design rights, confidential information and trade secrets. For other IPRs, registration with the competent authorities is required to establish legal title over the IPR. If no registration occurs, third parties are generally free to register and use your creations. This includes patents, trademarks and industrial designs.

For foreign investors, the following shows the most relevant IPRs in practice:

IPR Type	Description	Protection Duration
Trademark	Marks used to distinguish goods or services of different organisations and individuals. They may take the form of words, images or any combination.	10 years from the date of application, renewable for successive 10-year periods without limitation.
Patent	A technological solution presenting worldwide novelty, an inventive step applicable in socio-economic fields.	20 / 10 years from the date of application for invention / utility solutions patents.
Industrial Design Patent	The outward appearance of a product embodied in three-dimensional configuration, lines, colours or a combination of such elements.	5 years from the date of application, renewable twice for 5 years each, up to a maximum of 15 years.
Copyright	Rights of an organisation or individual to works which such organisation or individual created or owns. "Works" means a creation of the mind in the literary, artistic or scientific sectors, expressed in any mode or form.	50 years after author's death. 75 years for films, photos, literary works, works of applied art and anonymous works.
Trade Secret	Information obtained illegally from business / investment activities, which has not priorly been disclosed.	Recognized but only if both violation and specific damages can be evidenced.

6.2 Registration

All registrations of IPRs must be made at the National Office of Intellectual Property Rights (NOIP), which is a subsidiary organisation of the Ministry of Science and Technology. The NOIP's preliminary examination of applications must be completed within three months after receipt. After this, there will be a further evaluation lasting for at least nine months. In practice, IPR registration can take up to 18 months.

6.3.1 Trademarks

Trademarks can be protected by the IP Law if they are distinctive, visible signs in form of letters, words, drawings or images including holograms, or a combination of these, represented in one or more colours. A trademark is distinctive if it consists of one or more easily noticeable and memorable elements or a combination thereof. Three-dimensional signs (shapes) can be registered as trademarks, but trademarks based on sound and smell are not recognized.

Trademark protection lasts for 10 years from the approval date of the NOIP and can be extended for consecutive 10-year periods for an unlimited number of times. The IP-Law provides a number of circumstances under which a trademark is not eligible for protection, such as in case it is identical or confusingly similar to another trademark already registered or used for identical or similar goods or services in Vietnam.

IPRs are territorial in nature, which means that registrations in one country's jurisdiction are not automatically enforceable in others, and therefore registrations in multiple countries may be necessary. In practice, Foreign Investors often do not register their trademarks locally in Vietnam, because they believe to having already automatically obtained international trademark protection under the Madrid Agreement / WIPO system. However, Vietnam operates under a "first-to-file" system, meaning that the first person to file an IPR application at the NOIP for the territory of Vietnam will own that trademark once approved by the NOIP, regardless of whether or not an international registration under the Madrid Agreement already exists. The NOIP therefore disregards registration under the Madrid Agreement by allowing local registrations even where international protection has already been granted.

Because of the NOIP's above practical approach, it is essential to always register trademarks locally in Vietnam (either by trademark extension over WIPO or by initial trademark application in Vietnam), even if automatic protection under the Madrid Agreement should in theory be sufficient. Otherwise, any third party can register the trademark in Vietnam and then become for the territory of Vietnam the (illegal) owner of that trademark, despite Vietnam being a signatory to the Madrid Agreement. In these (not so uncommon) cases of "bad-faith" registrations, the real trademark owner is then blackmailed to buy back their own trademarks at an inflated price.

6.3.2 Patents

A patent is an exclusive right granted for an invention. A patent requires i) inventiveness, meaning a new technical solution or improvement to a product or process, ii) novelty, meaning it has not been published or disclosed to the public before, and iii) industrial applicability, meaning that it can be developed into mass manufacturing. Once the patent is granted, invention patents last 20 years without possibility for extension. Utility solution patents last 10 years without possibility for extension. The registration process for both often takes up to 20 months.

To obtain a patent for the territory of Vietnam, an application must be filed with the NOIP. As with trademarks, Vietnam operates under a "first-to-file" system, meaning that the first person to file a patent in Vietnam will own the IPR for Vietnam once the application is granted, regardless of whether another party was the inventor or the first user of the patented creation. With Vietnam being a party to the Paris Convention, applicants are entitled to a right of priority if the same filing has been made within the last 12 months in any other country being party to the convention. This is useful for patent owners because after first filing in their home country, they then have 12 months to decide which other countries they want to register in, before having to commence international filings.

6.3.3 Industrial Designs

An industrial design patent means a specific appearance of a product embodied by three-dimensional configurations, lines, colours, or a combination of these elements. Industrial design patents cover products with a distinctive shape, pattern or colour, which still maintain novelty and industrial applicability. In order for an industrial design patent to be granted, the design must be new, creative and have an industrial application. An industrial design patent is considered "new" if it differs substantially from industrial designs that are already disclosed to the public inside or outside Vietnam. An industrial design is deemed "creative" if it cannot easily be created by a person with average knowledge in the relevant field. Like patents, an industrial design is considered capable of industrial application if it can be used as a model for mass manufacture of products. However, these cases shall not be protected as industrial design patents: i) if the appearance of a product is dictated by the technical features of the product, ii) the appearance of a civil or an industrial construction work, iii) the shape of a product if it is invisible during product use. Industrial design patents last 5 years, with the option to extend twice for consecutive 5-year periods (15-year maximum protection). Registration may take up to 18 months.

6.3.4 Trade Secrets

Trade secrets include information obtained from financial or intellectual investment activities, which have not been disclosed and are applicable in business. Information qualifies as a trade secret if the information i) has not been made to the public and is therefore not common knowledge, ii) gives its owner a business advantage and iii) remains secret because the owner takes necessary measures to protect the confidentiality of the information. Examples for trade secrets include new products or business models, special techniques, customer and supplier lists, technical know-how etc. Trade secrets do not include personal secrets, state management secrets and other confidential information which is not relevant to business. In practice, trade secrets are protected upon creation and cannot be registered with the NOIP. However, despite being unregistered rights, trade secrets are increasingly being recognized in Vietnam. They can, at least in theory, be enforced provided their owner can evidence that they are non-public, have commercial value, and sufficient measures have been taken to protect their confidentiality. Those measures include, amongst others, restricting employees' and third parties' access to trade secrets, marking documents with trade secrets as confidential and protecting trade secrets by confidentiality and non-disclosure agreements with employees and third parties wherever possible.

6.3.5 Copyrights

Vietnamese IP Law protects literary, artistic and scientific works (including performances, audio and visual fixation, broadcasts and satellite signals carrying coded programmes) such as e.g. literary works, scientific works, textbooks, teaching materials, lectures and speeches, press articles, musicals, films and photos, art works, drawings, sketches, plans, maps and architectural works, computer programs and data collections.

Protection duration is 75 years from publication for cinematographic works, photographic works, dramatic works, works of applied art and anonymous works, and 50 years after the death of the author for other works.

In Vietnam, copyrights are automatically protected under the Berne Convention which extends protection to all treaty countries. However, copyright registration is still advisable to obtain copyright certificates which serve as documentary evidence in case IPR enforcement becomes necessary. Registrations are filed at the National Copyright Office.

6.3 Enforcement

Qualification levels of court officials, judges, customs authorities and other IPR enforcement agencies are still relatively low. Specifically, IPR enforcement agencies outside the big cities often lack both experience and training to render fair decisions and judgements in line with Vietnamese law. Moreover, victims to IPR violations must provide documentary evidence proving the IPR infringement(s) and the actual damages suffered as a consequence of such infringement.

Administrative Actions: Administrative action is the most common route when dealing with IPR infringements. As administrative agencies still lack the expertise to resolve complex disputes, expert opinions must often be obtained to facilitate the resolution of the case. Depending on the value and nature of the case, different governmental bodies may be involved, such as the e.g., the police, customs market control force and competition authority. Those bodies are able to issue on the IPR infringer different penalties and sanctions such as "cease- and desist" orders, fines up to VND 500 million, confiscation and/or destruction of infringing goods as well as means for producing the infringing goods, suspension of infringer's business license, removal of infringing elements from a product, withdrawal of domain name and/or company's name containing infringing elements, recall of infringing goods already on the market and in some cases the recovery of illegal profit. A request to apply administrative measures against IPR infringers should be filed with the relevant enforcement authority and include with the application: i) documentary evidence of ownership of the infringed IPRs, ii) other evidence such as e.g., samples or photographs or the counterfeit/infringed goods, iii) proof of damages caused by the infringement (if possible) and iv) an expert opinion (if available). Upon submission of those documents, the enforcement agency in charge will then examine the request within one month from its filing date. If the request and its documentation are complete, the competent authority will then raid and seize infringing goods without prior notice to the infringer. If an infringement is found, the relevant authority will also impose sanctions and penalties upon the infringer.

Civil Litigation: For IPR holders to claim civil damages, they must commence civil litigation against the infringer. Damages are based on lost sales or the infringer's profits, however if the actual damages cannot be determined, the maximum amount the court can award in such cases is VND 500 million. By taking civil action, IPR holders may also request provisional measures (preliminary injunctions) and claim remedies available under law, especially claims for damages. IPR holders must file civil claims to the competent court within two years from the date of infringement discovery.

Criminal Prosecution: While IPR infringements may constitute a crime, pressing criminal charges against IRP infringers can be a challenging task, because court-proof evidence must be provided to the court and such evidence is often difficult to obtain. Also, a criminal conviction will not recover any civil damages or losses. Penalties for IPR infringements include monetary fines of up to VND 1 billion and imprisonment of up to three years, provided that the infringement is i) intentional, and ii) on a 'commercial scale'.

6.4 Licensing Agreements

Licensing of industrial property rights must be made by written contract ("Licensing Agreement"). The following licensing restrictions exist:

- The right to use geographical indications or trade names is not licensable.
- The right to use collective marks must not be licensed to organizations or individuals other than members of the owners of such collective marks.
- The licensee must not enter into a sub-licence contract with a third party unless it is so permitted by the licensor.
- Trademark licensees are obliged to indicate on goods and goods packages that such goods have been manufactured under mark licence contracts.

The IP Law recognizes the following types of Licensing Agreements:

1. ***Exclusive Licensing Agreement***: An agreement under which the licensee shall have the exclusive right to use the licensed industrial property object while the licensor may neither enter into any industrial property object licence contract with any third party nor, without permission from the licensee, use such industrial property object.
2. ***Non-exclusive Licensing Agreement:*** An agreement under which, within the licensing scope and term, the licensor shall still have

the right to use the industrial property object and to enter into a non-exclusive industrial property object licence contract with others.

3. ***Sub-licence Licensing Agreement*** means an agreement under which the licensor is a licensee of the right to use such industrial property object pursuant to another contract.

Licensing Agreements must contain at least the following content:

- Full names and addresses of the licensor and of the licensee,
- Agreement type and term, licensing price and grounds,
- Licensing scope, rights use and territorial limitations, and
- Licensor and licensee rights and obligations.

A Licensing Agreement must not include provisions which "unreasonably restrict the right of the licensee", which are considered automatically invalid. These include:

- prohibiting the licensee from improving the industrial property object other than marks;
- compelling the licensee to transfer free of charge to the licensor improvements of the industrial property object made by the licensee or the right of industrial property registration or industrial property rights to such improvements;
- Directly or indirectly restricting the licensee from exporting goods produced or services provided under the industrial

property object licence contract to the territories where the licensor neither holds the respective industrial property right nor has the exclusive right to import such goods;

- Compelling the licensee to buy all or a certain percentage of raw materials, components or equipment from the licensor or a third party designated by the licensor not for the purpose of ensuring the quality of goods produced or services provided by the licensee;
- Prohibiting the licensee from complaining about or initiating lawsuits with regard to the validity of the industrial property rights or the licensor's right to license.

6.5 Practical Tips

- ***Register your IPRs locally in Vietnam:*** Even if you have already registered in another Madrid Agreement country.
- ***Avoid sharing or disclosing IPRs with business- or JV partners:*** Only share if absolutely necessary and only after having carried out a comprehensive risk assessment.
- ***Include IPR protection clauses in your employment contracts:*** Always include in your employment contracts effective IPR protection clauses and educate your employees on the importance

of IPR protection, specifically though compliance trainings and assigning one staff to IPR protection.

- ***Have IPR protection procedures and mechanisms in place:*** Have sound physical protection and destruction methods for documents, drawings, tooling, samples, machinery etc. to avoid leakages of IPRs to third parties and/or competitors.
- ***Check market competitors:*** Make sure that your genuine products are not re-sold under a different brand name. Only use reliable distribution partners with clear distribution agreements.
- ***Use experience of established companies:*** Where possible, talk to other businesses already doing similar business in Vietnam about their experiences with protecting their IPRs in Vietnam. Talk in addition with experts and advisors such as lawyers and IP agents who can advise you on various courses of action to protect your IPRs and/or defend your IPRs.
- ***Pre-check your IPR status before entering Vietnam:*** Check whether someone has already registered your trademark in Vietnam, and if so, what course of action is recommended.
- ***Collect all evidence to protect your rights:*** Regarding enforcement, collect all evidence, specifically quotations, contracts with the infringing party and all email contains infringing information and all other documentary evidence.

7. Data Protection

7.1 Scope and Categories

The protection of personal data is governed by Decree No. 13/2023/ND-CP on Personal Data Protection (DPDP) a comprehensive legal framework for the protection of personal data. The DPDP now addresses in one decree all legal aspects of collecting, transferring, storing and processing personal data in Vietnam.

According to Article 49 DPDP, micro- and small enterprises, medium enterprises and start-up enterprises are allowed to choose to be exempt from the regulations on personal designation and personal data protection for a period of the first two years since the establishment of the business, however except for micro- and small enterprises, medium enterprises, start-up enterprises directly engaged in personal data processing activities.

7.1.1 Terminology

The DPDP introduces terminology similar to the EU General Data Protection Regulation (GDPR), as follows:

- ***Personal Data Controller:*** An organisation / individual deciding on purpose(s) and means by which personal data is processed.

- ***Personal Data Processor:*** An organisation or individual processing data on behalf of the data controller through a contract or agreement with the data controller.
- ***Personal Data Controlling and Processing Entity:*** An organisation or individual deciding the purpose(s) and means of processing personal data, as well as directly processes personal data.
- ***Third Party:*** An organisation or individual, other than the data subject, Data Controller, Data Processor and Personal Data Controlling and Processing Entity, that is permitted to process personal data.

Accordingly, the DPDP applies for all legal entities that are directly or indirectly involved in or related to personal data processing operations in Vietnam, including i) Vietnamese agencies, organizations and individuals; ii) Foreign agencies, organizations and individuals in Vietnam; iii) Vietnamese agencies, organizations and individuals operating abroad; and iv) Foreign agencies, organizations and individuals directly participating in or related to personal data processing activities in Vietnam.

7.1.2 Types of Personal Data

The DPDP divide personal data into basic personal data and sensitive personal data as follows:

Basic personal data: includes standard personal data that generally will not affect an individual's privacy, specifically the data subject's:

- full name, nationality, sex, marital status, place and date of birth date, death or disappearance, personal image;
- permanent, temporary and current residence, phone number;
- personal identification number (ID-card number), passport number, driver's license and license plate; and
- tax code; social and health insurance number.

Sensitive personal data: includes personal data associated with an individual's privacy that, if violated, will directly affect an individual's rights and interests, specifically:

- Political and religious beliefs;
- Health status and personal information stated in health records, excluding however information on the blood type;
- Racial or ethnic origin;
- Genetic data related to an individual's inherited or acquired genetic characteristics;
- Physical attributes and biological characteristics;
- Sex life or sexual orientation;

- Data on crimes and criminal activities collected and stored by law enforcement agencies;
- Information on customers of credit institutions, foreign bank branches, payment service providers, and other licensed institutions, including customer identification as prescribed by law, accounts, deposits, deposited assets, transactions, organisations and individuals that are guarantors at credit institutions, bank branches, and payment service providers;
- Personal location identified via location services; and
- Other specific personal data as prescribed by law that requires special protection.

In case of processing sensitive personal data, any Data Processor must i) designate a data protection department and appoint a data protection officer and ii) exchange information about such department and officer with the Department of Cyber Security and Hi-Tech Crime Prevention under the Ministry of Public Security (DCHCP).

7.2 Consent Requirements

The DPDP contains strict consent requirements for the valid transfer, storage and processing of sensitive personal data. Prior to carrying out and throughout the personal data processing, both the personal data controller and the personal data processor require with regards to all data processing activities the consent of the data subject, unless otherwise provided by law. Art 13 DPDP allows partial consent.

The data subjects' consent will only be valid if it is voluntary and the data subject fully understands: *i) the type of personal data that will be processed, ii) the purpose(s) of the personal data processing, iii) the organisations and individuals that are entitled to process the data subject's personal data and iv) the rights and obligations of the data subjects.*

In order to balance the rights and interests of data subjects and public interests, Article 17 DPDP, similar to the provisions of the GDPR, provides the following exceptions where processing personal data without the consent of data subjects is permitted:

- In case of an emergency, in which it is necessary to immediately process relevant personal data to protect the life and health of the data subject or others (note that the burden of evidence is with the Personal Data Controller, the Personal Data Processor, the Controller or the third party processing such data);
- Cases of disclosure of personal data as prescribed by law;
- The processing of data by competent state agencies in the event of an emergency related to national defense, security, social order and safety, major disasters or dangerous epidemics

or when there is a risk of threat to security and national defense but not to the extent of declaring a state of emergency;

- To prevent and combat riots and terrorism, to prevent and combat crimes and violations of the law;
- To fulfill the contractual obligations of the data subject with relevant agencies, organizations and individuals as prescribed by law; and
- Serving the activities of state agencies as prescribed by law.

The data subject's mere silence or non-response is not considered as consent. The data subject's consent must be:

- *expressed clearly and specifically in writing, verbally, by ticking the consent box or through the syntax that reflects consent via text message, or by selecting a technique that reflects consent, or by performing another action that signifies consent by selecting consent settings or by other actions that demonstrate consent*
- *made for the same purposes. When there are multiple purposes, the Data Controller, Data Controlling, and Processing Entity shall list down the relevant purposes so that the data subjects may provide their consents to one or more purposes on the list; and*
- *expressed in a format that can be printed, or copied in writing, including in electronic or verifiable formats.*

7.3 Rights of Data Subjects

Article 9 of the DPDP provides the following rights of data subjects with regards to the processing of their personal data:

- to be informed about the personal data processing;
- to give or withdraw consent to personal data processing;
- to object to personal data processing;
- to restrict personal data processing;
- to access and delete personal data;
- to be provided with information about the data processing;
- to bring complaints, denounce, and initiate lawsuits; to claim compensation for damage; and the
- Right to self-defence in case of unlawful processing.

Article 13 DPDP establishes a strict deadline for the Data Controller to enforce certain rights of the data subjects. In particular, the Data Controller is required to implement the right to restrict data processing, and the right to object to data processing within 72 hours upon the receipt of the request of the data subject.

7.4 Prohibited Activities and Breaches

Article 23 DPDP obliges organisations and individuals to notify the DCHCP upon detecting the following cases:

- There is a breach of the law with respect to personal data;
- Personal data is processed for wrong purposes, not in accordance with the original agreement between the relevant data subject and the Data Controller, the Data Controlling and Processing Entity, or it violates the provisions of the laws;
- The data subject's rights are not properly protected or implemented; and
- Other cases as prescribed by law, such as e.g., i) processing personal data to create information and data to fight against the State of the Socialist Republic of Vietnam; ii) processing personal data to create information and data that affect national security, social order and safety, and legitimate rights and interests of other organizations and individuals; iii) obstructing personal data protection activities of competent authorities and iv) taking advantage of personal data protection activities to violate the law.

Any notification of above breaches must be delivered to the DCHCP within 72 hours upon the detection of any of the aforementioned breaches. In case of late notification, reason for late notification must be included.

According to Article 4 DPDP, agencies, organizations and individuals that violate regulations on protection of personal data may bedisciplined, administratively sanctioned, criminal handling according to regulations.

7.5 Data Protection Measures

In order to ensure the ability to protect personal data rights and prevent personal data breaches, Articles 26-28 DPDP stipulate personal data protection measures that must be applied during the transfer, storage and processing of personal data, including:

- Management measures taken by organizations and individuals related to the processing of personal data;
- Technical measures taken by organizations and individuals related to the processing of personal data;
- Measures taken by competent state management agencies in accordance with this Decree and relevant laws;
- Investigative and procedural measures taken by competent state agencies and other measures.

In case of data transfers to Vietnam, data processing entities in Vietnam (including FIEs) must take appropriate technical and organizational measures to

ensure the same level of data protection as in the country where the data subjects are located. For example, the GDPR specifically requires data processors in third countries (e.g., Vietnam), to implement suitable measures to ensure:

1. *The pseudonymization and encryption of personal data.*
2. *The ability to permanently ensure the confidentiality, integrity, availability and resilience of data processing systems and services.*
3. *The ability to rapidly restore the availability of personal data and access to them in the event of a physical or technical incident.*
4. *A process for the periodic review and evaluation of the effectiveness of the technical and organizational measures to ensure the security of the data processing.*

Additional technical and organisational measures (TORs): In addition to above "basic" TORs, data processing entities in Vietnam should regularly also address the following specific TORs:

- Accurate user identification and authorization.
- Protection of data during transmission.
- Protection of data during storage.
- Physical security of locations of data processing.
- Events logging.

- System configuration, including default configuration.
- Internal IT and IT security governance and management.
- Certification/assurance of processes and products.
- Data minimization.
- Data quality.
- Limited data retention.
- Accountability.
- Data portability and erasure.

Data Transfer Impact Assessments (DTIAs): Regarding the transfer of personal customer data from the EU to Vietnam, EU data exporters often request from data processors in Vietnam a DTIA to assess in detail country risk in Vietnam and identifying appropriate supplementary measures.

About the Author

Dr. Matthias Dühn, LL.M. (Georgetown) has been admitted as a German lawyer (Rechtsanwalt) since 2001 and as a foreign registered lawyer Vietnam since 2007. Dr. Dühn focuses his practice on foreign investment and market entry to Vietnam, corporate- and commercial law, complex contract drafting and negotiations, employment-related settlements and commercial litigation/arbitration. Dr. Dühn's experience covers numerous sectors and industries, such as e.g., sales and distribution, manufacturing, pharma, IT and business process outsourcing (BPO). His clients include mostly internationally operating SMEs as well as private entrepreneurs and individuals.

Prior to establishing Viet Diligence Legal, Dr. Dühn has gained relevant industry experience as the regional Chief Compliance Officer Asia-Pacific at MAN Truck & Bus based in Bangkok and Senior Legal Counsel for chipmaker Infineon Technologies. Dr. Dühn received his law degree from the Friedrich-Schiller University Jena and completed his PhD in 2003 at the University of Osnabrück. In 2005, Dr. Dühn also received a Master of Laws Degree (LL.M.) in Securities and Financial Regulation from the Georgetown University Law Center, Washington D.C.

You can reach the author at:

E-Mail: matthias.duehn@vietdiligence.com

Website: www.vietdiligence.com

Mobile / Whatsapp: +84(0) 914 247 295

Viet Diligence Legal (VDL) is a fully Vietnam-licensed law firm offering comprehensive, cost-effective and practice-oriented legal and tax advice in Vietnam. By truly understanding your entrepreneurial and commercial objectives, VDL delivers quality and added value through hands-on legal solutions that help you achieving your business objectives in Vietnam. We combine local expertise with the international experience of VDL's lawyers in Hanoi and Ho Chi Minh City. Our services include:

- ***Market entry Vietnam with a focus on foreign Direct Investment (FDI), company formations and Joint Ventures.***
- ***M&A transactions and advisory, including legal due diligence and restructurings.***
- ***Commercial transactions with a focus on complex international contract drafting, review and negotiation.***
- ***Vietnamese Labour Law, Employment- and HR compliance.***
- ***Vietnamese Real Estate and Construction Law, acquisition of apartments in Vietnam.***
- ***Family and Inheritance Law in Vietnam, with a focus on wealth preservation (prenuptial agreements and succession planning).***
- ***Commercial litigation in Vietnam, Arbitration proceedings at the Vietnam International Arbitration Centre (VIAC).***

Abbreviations

ASEAN	Association of South-East Asian Nations
BCC	Business Cooperation Contract
BOD	Board of Directors (of a JSC)
BOM	Board of Management (of a JSC)
CIT	Corporate Income Tax
DIA	Direct Investment Account
DOLISA	Department of Labour, Invalids and Social Affairs
DPDP	Decree on Data Protection
DPI	Department of Planning and Investment
DTA	Double Taxation Agreement
ERC	Enterprise Registration Cerificate
FCT	Foreign Contractor Withholding Tax
FIE	Foreign Invested Enterprise
GD	General Director
GMS	General Meeting of Shareholders
GDPR	EU General Data Protection Regulation
IIA	Indirect Investment Account
ILRs	Internal Labour Regulations
IPA	Investment Policy Approval
IRC	Investment Registration Certificate
JSC	Joint Stock Company
JV	Joint Venture
LAC	Labour Arbitration Council
LLC	Limited Liability Company

LOC	Competition Law No. 23/2018/QH14
LOE	Law on Enterprises No. 59/2020/QH14
LOI	Law on Investment No. 61/2020/QH14
LR	Legal Representative (of both LLC and JSC)
LUR	Land Use Right
LURC	Land Use Right Certificate
MC	Members' Council (of a LLC)
MLLC	Multiple Member LLC
MPS	Ministry of Public Security
DOIT	Department of Industry and Trade
DPI	Department of Planning and Investment
PIT	Personal Income Tax
PPP	Public Private Partnership
SIAC	Singapore International Arbitration Centre
SLLC	Single Member LLC
SST	Special Sales Tax
USD	United States Dollars
VCCI	Vietnam Chamber of Commerce and Industry
VIAC	Vietnamese International Arbitration Centre
VAS	Vietnamese Accounting Standards
VAT	Value Added Tax
VLC	Vietnam Labour Code
VND	Vietnam Dong
WTO	World Trade Organization

Printed in Poland
by Amazon Fulfillment
Poland Sp. z o.o., Wrocław